Mary A. Lathbury

Child's Life of Christ

Stories from the Bible

Mary A. Lathbury

Child's Life of Christ
Stories from the Bible

ISBN/EAN: 9783337100063

Printed in Europe, USA, Canada, Australia, Japan

Cover: Foto ©Lupo / pixelio.de

More available books at **www.hansebooks.com**

CHILD'S
LIFE OF CHRIST

Stories from the Bible

THE HOLY CHILD AND THE WISE MEN.

CHILD'S
LIFE OF CHRIST

Stories from the Bible

BY

MARY A. LATHBURY

WITH INTRODUCTION BY

BISHOP JOHN H. VINCENT

ILLUSTRATED

WITH NUMEROUS FULL-PAGE COLORED PLATES,
AND PHOTO-ENGRAVINGS

Boston
DeWolfe, Fiske & Co.

PREFACE.

To Mothers.

I HAVE been asked to prepare this little aid for your use in the Home—that first and greatest of schools. The school was founded by the Maker of men, and He called mothers to be its earliest and most important teachers. He prepared a text-book for it which we call His Word, illustrating it richly and fully from life and Nature, and filling it with His Spirit. Wherever it is known, as the children become the members of the Church, the citizens of the State, the people of the World, the Book goes with them, forming the Church, the State, the World. It is not only equal to the need, but contains infinite riches that wait to be unveiled.

That no busy mother may say, "I cannot take time to gather from the Bible the simple lessons that my children need," this book of little stories—together making one—has been written. I have tried to preserve the pure outlines of the sacred record from the vivid description and the suggestive supposition that are sometimes introduced to add charm to the story, and in all quoted speech I have used the exact words of the authorized version of the Scriptures, so that the earliest impression made upon the memory of the child might be one that should remain.

The stories are not a substitute for the Word—only little approaches to it through which young feet may be guided by her who holds a place next to the great Teacher in His work with little children.

M. A. L.

INTRODUCTION.

WHEN the children gather at mother's knee, and the tiniest finds a place in mother's arms, and all clamor for a "story," "a story, mamma," how lovely is the picture—the living picture—that circle makes! Love, longing, wisdom, expectancy, faith, shining eyes, lips that move involuntarily, keeping time to the sweet movements of mother's lips! Blessed group! Happy mother!

When the stories mother tells are light and meaningless, full of rhyme and rollick, even their eyes are bright and faces radiant, and her own sweet face and voice give charm and weight and significance to the delicious nonsense she rehearses.

Why not give to this receptive and eager audience stories full of deepest meaning, facts, parables, myths charged with *truth*? Why not people little memories with heroes, saints, kings, prophets, apostles? Why not give stories to story-loving youngsters that will turn into immortal pictures and be transformed some day into living factors in the making of character? And why not give them as comparison the babe of Bethlehem, the boy of Nazareth, the lad of twelve years in the schools of the Temple, the man of gentle love, the preacher of righteousness, the worker of heavenly wonders, the Son of Man, the Son of God, the Prince of Peace?

The Book of books is the children's Book. It is a story book. And the stories are "true stories." And the lessons to be drawn from them are numberless, and will come up out of the treasure-house of memory when mother's eyes are closed and her voice silent.

It is a great thing to put mother and the Book together in Baby's thought; in the big boy's memory; in the grown-up man's heart and life.

This book is mother's book; to aid her in doing the best and most lasting work a mother can do to sow seed and set out vines the branches of which shall reach into the world of spirits, and from which she and her children may long afterwards pluck fruit together in the eternal kingdom.

JOHN H. VINCENT.

CHAUTAUQUA, 1898.

CONTENTS.

CHAPTER		PAGE
I.	THE ANGELS OF THE ADVENT	1
II.	FOLLOWING THE STAR	5
III.	THE FLIGHT INTO EGYPT	7
IV.	THE BOY OF NAZARETH	11
V.	THE YOUNG CARPENTER	14
VI.	THE VOICE IN THE WILDERNESS	15
VII.	JESUS IN THE DESERT	18
VIII.	THE FIRST DISCIPLES	20
IX.	THE FIRST MIRACLE	22
X.	IN HIS FATHER'S HOUSE	24
XI.	A TALK ABOUT THE BREATH OF GOD	27
XII.	A TALK ABOUT THE WATER OF LIFE	28
XIII.	JESUS IN THE SYNAGOGUE	30
XIV.	AMONG THE FISHERMEN	34
XV.	THE HEALING HAND OF JESUS	35
XVI.	FOLLOWING JESUS	36
XVII.	FRIENDS OF JESUS	41
XVIII.	THE LORD OF LIFE	45
XIX.	MARY OF MAGDALA	46
XX.	STORIES TOLD BY THE LAKE	49
XXI.	STILLING THE STORM	52
XXII.	CALLED BACK	54
XXIII.	TWO BY TWO	57
XXIV.	WALKING THE WAVES—THE TWO KINGDOMS	62
XXV.	A JOURNEY WITH JESUS	64
XXVI.	THE CHRISTIAN SABBATH—PETER'S CONFESSION OF FAITH	68
XXVII.	"AND WE BEHELD HIS GLORY"—A FATHER'S FAITH	72
XXVIII.	THE LORD AND THE LITTLE ONES—LEAVING GALILEE	74
XXIX.	AT THE HOUSE OF MARTHA—THE GOOD SHEPHERD	76
XXX.	THE LESSON STORIES OF JESUS	82

CONTENTS.

CHAPTER.		PAGE.
XXXI.	THE VOICE THAT WAKED THE DEAD—THE CHILDREN OF THE KINGDOM	86
XXXII.	THE YOUNG MAN THAT JESUS LOVED	91
XXXIII.	THE LAST JOURNEY TO JERUSALEM	92
XXXIV.	THE PRINCE OF PEACE	94
XXXV.	THE CHILDREN IN THE TEMPLE	95
XXXVI.	THE LAST DAY IN THE TEMPLE	96
XXXVII.	THE LAST WORDS IN THE TEMPLE	98
XXXVIII.	AN EVENING ON THE MOUNT OF OLIVES	102
XXXIX.	THE HOLY SUPPER	103
XL.	THE NIGHT OF THE BETRAYAL	106
XLI.	DESPISED AND REJECTED OF MEN	110
XLII.	THE KING OF HEAVEN AT THE BAR OF PILATE	113
XLIII.	LOVE AND DEATH	116
XLIV.	LOVE AND LIFE	120
XLV.	THE EVENING OF EASTER	124
XLVI.	THE LORD'S LAST DAYS WITH HIS DISCIPLES	127
XLVII.	"HE ASCENDED INTO HEAVEN"	130
XLVIII.	THE PROMISE OF THE FATHER	132
AN AFTERWORD		134

COLORED ILLUSTRATIONS.

THE HOLY CHILD AND THE WISE MEN	.	Frontispiece
IN HIS FATHER'S HOUSE	.	Opposite Page 11
AT JACOB'S WELL		" " 26
THE NET FULL OF FISHES		" " 36
JESUS IN THE STORM		" " 46
THE LITTLE GIRL WHO WAS CALLED BACK		" " 54
JESUS WALKING UPON THE WAVES		" " 66
THE MOTHERS OF JERUSALEM		" " 76
"JESUS WEPT"		" " 86
"HOSANNA!"		" " 96
THE HOLY SUPPER		" " 106
"ART THOU A KING?"		" " 116

CHILD'S LIFE OF CHRIST.

STORIES FROM THE BIBLE.

CHAPTER I.

THE ANGELS OF THE ADVENT.

THERE was an old priest named Zacharias, who lived in the hill country of Hebron, where Abraham the father of the Jewish people used to live. He went to Jerusalem when it was his turn to serve in the temple, and once while he was offering the incense of sweet spices on the golden altar, he saw through the rising smoke an angel standing on the right side of the altar. The good priest was frightened, but the angel said,

"Fear not, Zacharias, for thy prayer is heard," and he promised that to him and his wife Elizabeth should be born a little son, whose name should be John. He was coming to prepare the way for the Messiah, and must not drink wine or strong drink, for he was to be filled with the Holy Spirit.

It was too wonderful for Zacharias to believe, and when he went out of the temple he was dumb, and all the people who waited for him knew that he had seen a vision. He did not speak while he stayed to minister in the temple, and when his time of service was ended he went to his home in Hebron.

A few months later the angel Gabriel went to the little town of Nazareth, high up among the hills of Galilee, and spoke to a young girl named Mary. She had never seen an angel, and she also was afraid when he said to her,

"Hail, thou that art highly favored, the Lord is with thee; blessed art thou among women. Fear not, Mary, for thou hast found favor with God." And then he told her that she should become the mother of a Holy Child, who should also be the Son of the Highest, and a King whose kingdom should have no end, and His name should be Jesus. He also told her of her cousin Elizabeth away in Hebron, to whom a little son was promised.

Then Mary said these beautiful words to the angel:

"Behold the hand-maid of the Lord; be it unto me according to Thy word," and the angel went away into heaven.

Mary was so full of wonder at the angel's words that she set out on a journey to see Elizabeth. It was eighty miles to Hebron, but it was early summer, and as Mary went through the green valleys and fruitful plains, and along by the flowing Jordan, she thought about the angel's words, and prayed to God to make her good and wise. She was not afraid, though the journey was four days long, for she knew God was with her.

On the fourth day she passed Jerusalem, the Holy City, and went on and up into the Hebron Hills to the house of Elizabeth. When they told to each other the wonderful words of the angel Gabriel they were full of joy, for they knew that the coming of the Christ was near, and that the Lord had trusted them with the heavenly secret. They were filled with the Holy Spirit, and Mary broke out into a beautiful song of praise.

Mary stayed three months with her cousin Elizabeth, and learned many things, for the old priest and his wife were wise and good. When she went back to Nazareth she told no one of her vision, not even her mother or Joseph, the good carpenter, whose promised wife she was. But the angel came one night to Joseph and spoke to him through a dream of the Holy Child that was to be born.

Now Joseph and Mary were of the family of King David, and they knew that the prophets had long ago talked of a King who was to come and restore the kingdom, and reign on the throne of David. They even told where he was to be born, in Bethlehem, the "City of David." And though the Jews had become the servants of the Romans, yet it was time, according to the promise, that the new King should come and set them free, and many were looking for His coming.

Perhaps Joseph and Mary thought of these things when the time came for them to go to Bethlehem, for the Emperor of Rome had made a decree that all Jews should be enrolled, that he might know how many were in his empire. So all Jews, who had gone to live in other parts, returned to their own tribe and city to be enrolled among their own people.

When Joseph and Mary came to Bethlehem they found it full of people who had also come home to write their names for the Emperor, and there was no room for them in the inn. It was winter, and while Joseph wondered what he should do the keeper of the inn showed them the stable where the gentle oxen and asses were kept, and where it was much quieter than in the noisy yard and crowded rooms of the inn.

It was here in a humble stable that the Lord of Heaven was born upon earth, and cradled in a manger. He chose the stable instead of a palace, and a bed of straw instead of a bed of down, for He had come to be the Brother of the poor and the Saviour of the world.

Out in the fields near by were some shepherds watching their flocks. It has been said that the flocks kept in the Bethlehem fields were for the sacrifices in the temple, and were watched night and day the year long, while other flocks were kept in their folds in winter.

While they sat on the rocks, wrapped in their cloaks and sheepskin jackets, with a fire of brushwood to keep the beasts away, perhaps they thought of young David, who once kept his sheep there, and killed a lion and a bear to defend his flock; or they watched the stars and wondered at their beauty.

But suddenly an angel stood by them, and a great light shone round about them, and they were terrified. But the angel spoke kindly to them saying:—

"Fear not, for behold I bring you good tidings of great joy, which shall be to all people. For unto you is born this day, in the city of David, a Saviour which is Christ the Lord." And the angel told them how they would know it to be the Holy Child—because it lay in a manger. Then, in a moment the air was full of angel faces, and heavenly voices sang this song of praise to God and promise to all people:—

"Glory to God in the highest, and on earth peace, good will toward men!" And they went away into heaven.

The shepherds looked at one another and then one said; "Let us go to Bethlehem." And they went in great haste. There they found Mary and Joseph with the Holy Child lying in a manger, just as the angel had said. They told the people of Bethlehem about the angels they had seen and the words they had heard, and they were very much astonished. But Mary was silent, and kept all these things in her heart to think about and to pray about.

As for the shepherds they went back to their flocks praising God.

When the Holy Child was eight days old his parents called His name Jesus, as the angel had commanded, and they dedicated him to the Lord. Later they took him up to the Temple at Jerusalem to make the offering that all Jewish mothers made, some money, if it was the first boy-child, and a lamb, or a pair of doves. Joseph bought for Mary a pair of doves, and they went up the white steps of the beautiful porch of the Temple, and passed the long rows of marble pillars into the court of the Gentiles where they could look up and see the Temple itself with its white marble pillars and golden roof shining in the sun.

Mary gave her doves to the Priest at the gate of the Court of the Women, and he took them away to be offered on the altar, while Joseph took the Holy Child into the Men's Court for the Priest to bless as he dedicated Him to the Lord. When all was done and they were going away, an old man named Simeon saw them, and begged to hold the child. He was a good man who had longed to see the Christ who was to come, and now the Spirit of God told him that this was He. He thanked God, and said:

"Lord, now lettest Thou thy servant depart in peace, according to Thy word, for mine eyes have seen Thy salvation."

He also spoke as a prophet of the days to come, and just then a very old woman who lived in the Temple, Anna, the prophetess, came and gave thanks to God, and told the people that the Redeemer had come to Israel. All these things Mary kept in her heart, as she had kept the words of the angel, and wondered why she had been chosen to be the mother of the Holy Child.

Seven months before this time a little son had been born to Zacharias and Elizabeth. The neighbors wished to name him for his father, but Elizabeth said, "Not so; but he shall be called John." When they asked his father what it should be, he wrote an answer (for he had been dumb ever since he talked with the angel in the Temple) and they read, "His name shall be called John." Then his mouth was opened, and he began to speak and to praise God, and his friends wondered what the child would be when he grew to manhood. His father became a prophet for a time, and said some strange things about him that were written down. He said that John should be called a prophet of the Highest, and go before the Lord to prepare His ways.

John grew, and he also grew strong in spirit, and while he was yet young he went to live in the deserts where he was taught of God to be a prophet and a preacher.

CHAPTER II.

FOLLOWING THE STAR.

While Joseph and Mary and the Holy Child were still staying in Bethlehem, some Wise Men came from and Eastern country to Jerusalem, asking,

"Where is he that is born King of the Jews? for we have seen His Star in the East, and are come to worship Him."

No one knows who these men were, but it may be that they were Jews who lived in Persia, as David had done long before, and were learned in all the wisdom of the Chaldeans, who studied the stars, and believed that they had much to do with the lives of people on the earth. These wise men were called Magi. They had heard that a great One would be born about this time, and that He would be the King of the Jews.

When they saw a strange and beautiful Star near the earth away toward Jerusalem they prepared to go and see if it would lead them to the King. Their servants loaded the camels with food and water and some costly gifts, for they were rich men, and mounted on beautiful saddles covered with blue and crimson cloth they rode away toward Jerusalem. They had deserts of yellow sand to cross, and they were tired at the end of the hot day, but at night they saw the beautiful Star shining before them low in the sky, and watched it from their tents on the sand where they rested for the night, and rose to follow it before it faded in the morning. They were glad when they came to the fresh green mountain country of the Jews, and rode through the flowery valleys till they came to the gates of Jerusalem. Perhaps they expected to hear all about the new King, and to find the people feasting and rejoicing, but they did not.

When they asked, "Where is He that is born King of the Jews?" the people were surprised, and only wondered who these men were who looked liked princes from a foreign court, for they had armed servants, and from their camels hung tinkling silver bells, and swinging tassels of silk and gold.

They searched Jerusalem for the king, and Herod heard of it and was troubled. He wished always to be king himself. He set the scribes to searching for the prophecies of the Messiah's birth. They knew very well where to find them, and they read to the king these words from the prophet Micah:—

FOLLOWING THE STAR.

"But thou, Bethlehem Ephratah, which art little among the families of Judah, out of thee shall One come forth unto me that is to be the ruler of Israel; whose goings forth are from of old, from ancient days."

Then the king sent for the wise men, for he had a secret plan. They came in their best robes, hoping perhaps, to find the newly born King in the beautiful palace of Herod on Mount Zion, but they found only the gloomy old King Herod waiting for them. He asked them when they first saw the Star, and when they had told him, he sent them to Bethlehem and said,

"Go and search diligently for the young child, and when ye have found him, bring me word again, that I may come and worship him also."

They were very glad to hear about Bethlehem, and as they came down the marble steps of Herod's palace it was evening, and there, low down before them in the sky was the Star! They went out through the Bethlehem gate toward the south, and followed the Star again over the hills until the white walls of Bethlehem shown in the moonlight before them, and they saw the Star standing still and shining down upon a little house within the walls. Then they rejoiced with exceeding great joy, for they had come to the end of their long journey, and they had found the King! When they came to the house where Mary and Joseph were staying they told their servants to unpack the presents of gold, and frankincense, and myrrh, and they went in. Then they found the lovely young mother and the Holy Child, and they fell down before Him and offered their gifts.

They did not go away at once. They slept in Bethlehem that night, and the Lord showed them in a dream that they must not go back to tell King Herod that they had found the Christ. They told Joseph of their dream, and went away by another road that led past Hebron to their own country.

CHAPTER III.

THE FLIGHT INTO EGYPT.

It seems very strange that in a few hours after the wise men had gone over the hills to their own country, that Mary and Joseph and the Holy Child should be swiftly following the same road. The night after the wise men had been warned in a dream to go to their own country, Joseph was warned also

THE FLIGHT INTO EGYPT.

in a dream to take the young Child and His mother and go into Egypt. He was told to stay until he had orders to return, for Herod would seek to take the Child's life. Their flight was in the night, and Mary's heart beat fast as she held her baby close and rode down the steep path from Bethlehem with Joseph walking beside her. They did not rest until they were far on their way. It was nearly a week before they reached the river that was the border of Egypt, but when they crossed it King Herod's soldiers could not harm them.

They had gold that the wise men had given them, and Joseph knew how to make many things of wood, so they lived quietly in Egypt waiting until the Lord should call them back.

Herod was very angry when he heard that the Magi had gone away without telling him anything about the young King; so angry that he ordered his soldiers to destroy every baby boy in Bethlehem. So all the little boys of Bethlehem under two years of age were killed by the order of this wicked king, and the Holy Child whom Herod believed would be destroyed with them was safely borne in His mother's arms along the road to Egypt, while Joseph walked beside them and led the patient ass, and angels went with them unseen to be their guard by night and by day.

They lived in Egypt about a year, and then the sick and unhappy old king died, and an angel came to Joseph one night in a dream, and said,

"Arise and take the young Child and His mother and go into the land of Israel, for they are dead which sought the young Child's life."

They were glad to know that they could come home again, and they came, perhaps with a company of merchants, into their own land. Joseph would have settled in Judea, the part of the land of Israel in which stands Jerusalem, and Bethlehem, the city of his ancestors, but Herod's son had been made king over Judea, and Joseph was told in a dream to go into Galilee.

In Galilee was Nazareth, where both Joseph and Mary lived when they were married, and there they went and were at home again, and there Jesus grew to manhood.

IN HIS FATHER'S HOUSE.

CHAPTER IV.

THE BOY OF NAZARETH.

Nazareth was a little town high among the hills of Galilee. It still stands there, but it is not so large a town as it was when Mary and Joseph and the Child Jesus lived there. Then Galilee was full of cities and villages, and men and women were busy among its fields, and vineyards, and gardens, and the shores of the beautiful Lake of Galilee were lined with the boats of fishermen.

Nazareth was more quiet than the crowded cities by the Lake. A great green plain lay below it, and a narrow road winding among the limestone rocks led up to it. Its streets were narrow and steep, and steps of stone led from house to house. A fountain of pure water breaking out of a rock was the meeting place of the women of Nazareth, who came with their tall pitchers for water and bore them away upon their heads. Here Mary often came tenderly leading the Holy Child. Perhaps He gathered the bright wild flowers that grew thick around the fountain and along the stream flowing from it. When he grew a little older He could climb the rocks around His home, or go with His mother and Joseph to the top of the hill from which they could see the snowy peak of Hermon, or the long line of shining blue sea beyond the hills on the west, or they would point out a slowly moving caravan of heavy-laden camels from Tyre and Sidon by the sea on their way to Damascus.

Sometimes He would go with Joseph to the woods when a certain piece of wood was needed, for Joseph was a carpenter, and in a lower room of his humble house of rough white stone there was a long bench and the tools of a wood-worker. Here, perhaps, the Holy Child played with the curled shavings that fell from the bench, and watched the making of the plows, the yokes, the doors, and the lattices until He was old enough to help in the making of them.

He learned to read and write while a young child at home, as Jewish children did, and His reading book was the Old Testament, which was the Jews' Bible. Then He went to school at the Synagogue, which was the Jews' Church, and there, we may be sure, He was a gentle, obedient pupil, and a loving, unselfish playmate. While he read He may have had many strange thoughts about the prophecies in the Book that were promises of the Messiah, the King that was to reign in righteousness.

When He was twelve years old His parents took Him with them to the Feast of the Passover at Jerusalem. Great companies of people went from all parts of the Jews' country, and from every country in which they had settled, to keep the feast that the Lord had commanded when they were led out of Egypt. The very journey to Jerusalem was a festival, for their friends joined the company from almost every house in Nazareth, and on horses, and camels, and asses, the men walking beside them, a happy group set forth from home to keep the Passover week in the city of the great King. It was the first visit of the boy Jesus to Jerusalem, and as He walked strong and beautiful beside Joseph, what tender and holy thoughts, what questions about the future must have filled the mind of Mary. He was going to see His Father's House, the beautiful Temple where the thousands of Israel gathered every year for worship and of which He had read in the Book of the Law, for He was now old enough to be called a "Son of the Law," and verses from the Bible folded in little boxes, had been tied upon his arm and his forehead by the village Rabbi, as a sign that He was old enough to think for Himself and go to the religious Feasts at Jerusalem.

When they reached the great public roads they found other companies of pilgrims going up to the Holy City, and by their banners they knew the tribe and city from which they came. There was music, also, of timbrel and pipe and drum as the songs of Zion were sung along the way, or at evening when they camped in the fields.

When they had climbed the steep Jericho road and the Mount of Olives, a glorious sight opened before them. There lay the City of David shining in the sun, its thick walls set with towers; its marble palaces, and castles, and gardens, and, most wonderful of all, the Temple with its hundreds of white marble pillars, its beautiful porches and arches, and, rising within its richly-paved courts, the Holy Place with the sun like fire upon its roof of gold. The people shouted and sang a song of joy. Perhaps they sang that song of David beginning:

> "I was glad when they said unto me
> ' Let us go into the house of the Lord, '
> Our feet shall stand within thy gates,
> O Jerusalem!"

Like thousands of others they pitched their tents outside of the walls, perhaps on the slopes of Olivet, and after eating the Passover supper together went daily into the Temple. To the Boy of Nazareth this must have been the one charmed spot in all Jerusalem. Other boys loved to watch the strange people from far countries, and wander among the bazars, but Jesus stayed in the Temple. He saw the white-robed priests, the altars, and the sacrifices; He saw the great curtains of purple and gold that hid the Holy place, and He heard the Temple choirs answer each other in song; He also saw the old Rabbis who taught and answered questions daily in the outer courts, and stood long among the listeners.

When the company from Nazareth began the journey home, and had gone as far as the plains of Jericho, Mary looked for her boy. She had not been troubled about him, for she thought He was walking with the other children, or with relatives, but when Joseph found that he was not with them they went back over the long, steep road full of fear and anxiety. They searched Jerusalem through, asking everybody they knew if they had seen the Boy Jesus.

When they had been searching for three days, and Mary's heart was almost broken, they went again to the Temple, and looking through a crowd gathered around the Rabbis, Mary saw her Boy. She pressed through to speak to Him, but He was speaking. She listened, and her heart must have stood still to hear His simple, yet wonderful words. Sometimes he asked questions which the old teachers could not answer, and when he replied to the questions of the learned teachers His wisdom astonished all who heard Him, for it was not like the wisdom of the Rabbis, who used many words to explain the Word of God.

When Jesus saw His mother and came to her, she said,

"Son, why hast Thou so dealt with us? Behold thy father and I have sought Thee sorrowing."

"How is it that ye sought me?" He said, "wist ye not that I must be about my Father's business?"

They did not quite understand how He could so easily forget them, and yet Mary, perhaps, remembered that the angel had told her that He should "be called the Son of God," and that He was at home in His Father's house.

But He was content to go home and be subject to His parents, so that through all the world children may learn how He lived, and try to live like Him.

He found that His Father's house was greater than the Temple, and under its starry roof, and wandering over its wide courts paved with grass and flowers, He learned more than the Rabbis could teach Him. And every day He grew in wisdom as He grew in stature, and "in favor with God and man."

CHAPTER V.

THE YOUNG CARPENTER.

There are many years of the life of Jesus of which the Gospel story tells us nothing. He lived with Mary and Joseph in Nazareth, and was preparing for the great work for which He came. He learned easily all that other boys were taught in the synagogue school, and no doubt caused His teacher to wonder at such wisdom coming from a boy. He was so humble and teachable that no one could accuse Him of setting Himself above His companions, and so winning and unselfish that He was loved by all. The school days ended, perhaps, when He was fourteen, and He was asked, as every Jewish boy was asked, to choose what trade He would learn, for every boy had to learn a trade. He chose to learn the trade of His father, and began to work with him making the many things that were then used by the people. Few houses, if any, were made of wood, for the white limestone was then, as now, used in making the houses of Nazareth, but they were finished with wood, and wood was used not only for boats, tables, benches, yokes and carts, but also for plows, saddles, and many things we now make of other material. Can you make a picture in your mind of this tall, beautiful youth standing near His father ready to serve in any humble way in the work they were doing?

There was no service so small that He did not willingly do it, and no labor so rough and common that He did not make it noble and beautiful by the doing. But He was always thinking—thinking. The world around Him was full of pictures and stories through which heavenly truths shone, and they formed themselves in His mind, and when He began to teach He used them to help others with. We call them parables. Wherever He saw the flowers, the grape vines, the olive and the fig trees, the wheat fields, the shepherds and their flocks, the fishermen and their nets, He read high and holy lessons that were much more simple, and true, and beautiful than those taught by the Rabbis.

The more He thought about the teaching of the Rabbis, the more He saw how false and hard it was. The Law given by Moses was full of the good thoughts of God, but the Jewish teachers had only taught the outward form, and had not given the people the inward spirit. It was like bringing to the hungry a beautiful dish with no food in it, or to the thirsty a costly cup with no water in it.

As He grew older He would sit sometimes long into the night on some hillside watching the stars, and with his great heart going out beyond the hills to the people of the world in longing love and in desire for their salvation. He wanted to show them how God loved the world. He wanted to take the empty forms of the Law and fill them full of the Spirit—the real thought and love of God. He wanted to take away the burdens on the minds of the people, which were heavier than those that Pharoah laid upon their bodies long before, and give them the rest and peace of God. He wanted to take away their endless rules and give them one rule—to do by others as they would have others do to them. And He wanted to add a new Commandment to the Law—that they love one another.

In this way, by living with His mind in heaven and His body on earth He came to know that He was the Christ of God, and that He must go out from Nazareth to be a Teacher of Truth, and begin to build The Kingdom of Heaven among men. But His friends thought that He was fitted to be a Rabbi and teach in the Temple with the Doctors of the Law. He waited many years, caring for His mother and His younger brothers and sisters after the death of Joseph, and then He left Nazareth.

CHAPTER VI.

THE VOICE IN THE WILDERNESS.

Jesus was thirty years of age when He left Nazareth to begin His work as a Teacher of the Truth. It was the age set by the older teachers for a young man to begin his work.

His cousin John, the son of Elizabeth and Zachariah, was six months older than Jesus, and he had begun his ministry on the lower Jordan. While Jesus had been living quietly at Nazareth preparing for his work, John had been away in the wilderness beyond the Dead Sea alone with the Spirit of God. He was a prophet who could be taught by God only. When his time to speak came he came out of the wilderness to a place on the banks of the Jordan, just above Jericho, called The Fords. Many people crossed at this place, and he stood on a bank above the river crying, "Repent, for the Kingdom of Heaven is at hand."

Like those who had made a vow to the Lord, John had never cut his hair, he wore a coarse garment woven of camel's hair, and lived on the simple food of the wilderness—locusts and wild honey. He seemed never to think of himself, but always of One who was coming. He said that he was only a "Voice," preparing the way for the Messiah, as Isaiah had prophesied centuries before, and the "Messenger" that had been promised through Malachi.

"Behold I will send My messenger, and he shall prepare the way before me."

He did something which seemed new and strange to the people. He called them to a change of mind—a turning away from sin, and, as a sign that they had done so, he baptized them in the river Jordan. He was getting the people ready for the coming of Christ, who was to begin the Kingdom of Heaven on earth.

Thousands were flocking down to the river to hear the new prophet. They went from all parts of Palestine, and Jesus, knowing that his hour had come, went also. He wore a white tunic gathered at the neck and reaching to his feet, and on it the large blue mantle of thick stuff that was worn in cold weather, for it was in the winter of the year 31.

We cannot know all about His parting with His mother, and the three days' journey to the Fords of Jordan, but we know that He came and stood with others on the banks while John preached.

On this day John's words were different. He had said that the Christ was coming, but to-day he said,

"There standeth One among you whom ye know not, whose shoe's latchet I am not worthy to unloose."

After this Jesus came down to the water's edge to be baptized, and John, though he had not seen Jesus since he was a young boy, knew Him. Ready to fall at His feet, John cried,

"I have need to be baptized of Thee, and comest thou to me?"

Jesus replied in a low voice,

"Suffer it to be so now, for thus it becometh us to fulfill all righteousness," and so reverently John baptized his Master.

As Jesus stepped from the water's edge to the river bank a strange and beautiful thing happened. Out of the warm, blue sky a white dove came circling down around the head of Jesus, who stood silent in prayer. With eyes lifted to heaven He saw the dove, which was the form in which the

JOHN THE BAPTIST AT JORDAN.

Spirit of God descended upon Him, and John saw it also, and both heard a voice from heaven saying,

"*Thou art my beloved Son, in whom I am well pleased.*"

This was the answer to Jesus' prayer. Only Jesus and John understood the meaning of these words, for they heard with the spirit. To others it seemed like thunder out of a clear sky, and they were full of wonder about the strange young man who had been baptized with such a beautiful and singular sign following. They also remembered what John had said, that the Christ was now standing among them, and perhaps this was he! And they wondered what John meant when he said that though he baptized with water, the coming Christ would baptize them with the Holy Spirit and with fire.

It was of little use to wonder about the Messiah, however, unless they could remember and do all that John had said to them about being honest and true in their hearts, for that was the only way to prepare for the kingdom that was near at hand. He told the rich to share with the poor; the people who handled money to be honest, and the soldiers to harm no one with word or hand, and to be contented with their wages.

When they were willing to give up the sins that John showed them they took the sign of baptism from John, which meant that they wished to be washed from their sins, and begin life in a new way.

CHAPTER VII.

JESUS IN THE DESERT.

The people were looking for the promised Messiah, and would have welcomed John as the Christ if John had not always said "One mightier than I cometh." "I am not the Christ." The sign of the Dove filled them with new thoughts.

While they were thinking Jesus went up the river bank alone. The power of the spirit was upon Him, and His great work before Him, and He wished to go for a time as far as possible from every human being. He went into the wilderness—a wild desert country beyond the Dead Sea—not even wishing to talk with John, whose home was in the wilderness. Perhaps John looked after Him and longed to see and talk with Him, but Jesus had one great desire, to know Himself, and what His work was to be. He felt two natures within Him, the human and the divine, and before He began to teach He wanted to hear the voice of the Divine within Him as clear and strong as He had heard it that day from the skies.

The desert to which He went was not a waste of flat sand, like the African desert, but masses of rock with sand and dry grasses between, great cliffs of chalk and limestone rise a thousand feet above the gloomy gulfs of rock through which torrents run in the rainy season, but which are dry and oven-like in summer. One great cliff called Quarantana is now full of caves cut out of the face of the rock by men who have hoped to win heaven by suffering as Jesus did.

Jesus was thinking—thinking, His human nature being full of hopes, fears, and prayers; His divine nature being full of strength, promise, comfort. He did not think of food when He came, and there was none to be found. So resting at night in a cave, and wandering farther among the mountains by day, Jesus spent forty days in the wilderness of Judea. While there He was tried by the spirit of evil in every way known to human nature, and when all was over, and He had not yielded to sin, His mind was calm and ready for His work, for He knew He was the Son of God.

When He was hungry the tempter said, "If thou be the Son of God command this stone that it be made bread."

It would have been easy for Him to try His power, but He knew that He did not come into the world to use it for Himself, but for others, and so He answered in the words of the Bible,

"Thou shalt not live by bread alone, but by every word of God."

Then in a vision He seemed to be in the Holy City upon a tower of the Temple that stood over a deep valley, and the tempter speaking within Him, said,

"If Thou be the Son of God cast Thyself down, for it is written, 'He shall give His angels charge concerning thee, and in their hands they shall bear thee up, lest thou dash thy foot against a stone.' "

But Jesus knew that though the words were the words of God, the voice was the voice of the tempter, and He answered,

"Thou shalt not tempt the Lord thy God."

Then in a vision again He seemed to see, from the top of a very high mountain, all the kingdoms of the world spread out before Him with their kings, and armies, and cities; their beautiful homes and lovely women, and great men with their gold, and jewels, and precious works of art, and the tempter said,

"All these things will I give Thee if Thou wilt fall down and worship me."

Then all the Divine power in Jesus rose up against this evil whisper, and He said,

"Get thee hence, Satan; for it is written, 'Thou shalt worship the Lord thy God, and Him only shalt thou serve.'"

We shall never know all that Jesus suffered during this long time when He was away from His home in Nazareth, and away from every human being, tempted by evil, surrounded by wild beasts, and faint from hunger, but we know He won a great victory over evil for us. So he became the Elder Brother and Friend of all who are tempted.

After His long fast and struggle with the powers of evil, angels came and cared for Him, bringing heavenly strength and comfort, and He rose in that strength and came again into the valley of Jordan, and found that spring had come while he had been in the desert, and the willows were green by the river side. John was still preaching and baptizing, but was a little farther up the river at Bethabara.

As Jesus came near John pointed to Him and said to the people,

"Behold the Lamb of God, which taketh away the sin of the world. This is He. . . . And I knew Him not, but He that sent me to baptize with water, the same said to me, 'Upon whom thou shalt see the spirit descending and remaining on Him, the same is He which baptizeth with the Holy Ghost.'"

CHAPTER VIII.

THE FIRST DISCIPLES.

The next day while two men named John and Andrew were talking with John the Baptist, Jesus passed by, and again John said, "Behold the Lamb of God." These two men had been priests and disciples of John, but they turned and followed Jesus, and John was content to have them do so, for he sought no honor for himself. Jesus when he saw them following said,

"What seek ye?"

And they, hardly knowing what to say, and wishing very much to know Him, said,

"Rabbi, where dwellest thou?"

He did not reprove them for giving Him the honored name of *Master*, but said,

"Come and see."

How gladly they went! No one knows where or how He lived, but whether in a house, or in such a little tent as the people of that region now carry with them when they travel, it was a quiet place where these two men who were looking eagerly for the Kingdom of God could sit at the feet of Jesus and talk with Him. He was a young man like themselves, but there was a wonderful spirit in Him that made them feel like worshipping Him.

The first thing that Andrew did was to go and find his brother, Simon Peter. They were both fishermen from Bethsaida on Lake Galilee, and had come down to hear the new prophet John.

"We have found the Messiah!" said Andrew, and they both went back to Jesus.

When the Lord—for this He had been always—saw Simon Peter He saw his heart, and knew that he would be one of the founders of the kingdom with Him, and so He, looking straight through him, said,

"Thou art Simon, the son of Jona; thou shalt be called Cephas, which is by interpretation Peter." (A stone.)

So John, the loving; Andrew, the obedient, and Peter, the believing began to follow Jesus. And Peter's strong faith was like a foundation of stone in the beginning of the building of the kingdom.

There was another man from Bethsaida who had come down to hear John. His name was Philip. Jesus found him and said, "Follow Me." And he not only followed Jesus, but he went joyfully to find his friend, Nathanael, and tell him that they had found the Messiah, Jesus of Nazareth, the son of Joseph.

Nathanael could not believe that the Messiah would be a man of Nazareth, because the prophets had said that He would come from Bethlehem.

So he said, "Can any good thing come out of Nazareth?"

"Come and see," said Philip, urgently, and he went.

As he came to Jesus he met the deep, kind look that had searched Peter's heart and heard Jesus say,

"Behold an Israelite indeed, in whom there is no guile!" He saw innocence in the heart of Nathanael, but Nathanael wondered how Jesus could know him.

"Before that Philip called thee when thou wast under the fig-tree, I saw thee, said Jesus.

Then Nathanael's whole heart went over to Jesus, and he cried,

"Rabbi, Thou art the Son of God; Thou art the King of Israel!"

He needed nothing more to prove that Jesus was the Christ, but Jesus told him that he should see greater things, angels out of the open heaven ascending and descending upon Him.

Nathanael became the fifth disciple. His name was afterward called Bartholomew.

CHAPTER IX.

THE FIRST MIRACLE.

Jesus and the five who had become His constant friends and disciples, turned their faces toward home, for they were all from Galilee. It was Spring, and the land was beautiful with the fresh green of the trees and the breaking forth of wild flowers among the grass. On the journey the disciples scarcely saw the beauty around them, or felt weary from the journey, for they were hearing the gracious words of their new Friend concerning the coming in of the kingdom.

There was to be a marriage feast near Nazareth in the home of a friend. Mary and her family were invited, and also the friends who had come with Jesus. It was at Cana, a village between Nazareth and the lake, and they walked over the hills early to see the bride, crowned with flowers and a white veil, married to the man to whom she had given herself. Then followed a feast at the house of the father of the bridegroom. There were joyful greetings, and garlands of flowers, and wine—for Palestine was the land of vineyards, and they knew how to prepare a harmless wine. Before the feast was over they found that the wine had given out, and those who served the feast were distressed. It was thought a disgrace to fail in hospitality at a wedding feast, and so Mary came to Jesus for advice, saying,

"They have no wine."

"Woman," He said—and among the Jews this was a respectful manner of speaking to a woman—"what have I to do with thee? Mine hour is not yet come."

THE MARRIAGE AT CANA.

He meant that He must act from the Divine Nature, and not from the human nature that He had received from His mother.

"Whatsoever He saith unto you, do it," said Mary to the servants.

He told them to fill with water the six large water-pots of stone that stood near, and they filled them to the brim.

"Draw out now, and bear to the governor of the feast," He said, and it was served at the table, and the master of the feast called to the bridegroom,

"Thou hast saved the good wine until now."

This was the beginning of miracles.

These were happy days for Mary, for she had her Son back again. From the wedding Jesus and His mother, and His brothers, and His disciples went down to Capernaum by the lake for a few days.

Here Peter lived by the blue, beautiful lake that is walled by high hills on one side, while on the other lies what once was the "garden of Gennesaret" watered by streams, and rich with fruits, and grains, and flowers.

CHAPTER X.

IN HIS FATHER'S HOUSE.

The feeling that Jesus had when a boy, that He must be about His Father's business was now satisfied. He had begun the work of His ministry, though He had been doing all those silent years the tremendous work of overcoming evil for us. He met it in His own human nature, and overcame it step by step without yielding to sin. He was to do this work until it should be finished upon the cross, but for three years He was to teach the people the truths of the new kingdom, and show by His life, and at last by the laying down of His life, that love had come into the world to fill the old forms of the law full of the new Spirit of Life. He was to take away the sins of the world, and in place of them give to the world eternal life.

It was time for the Passover Feast again, and Jesus with his disciples joined the Capernaum company and started on the pleasant journey to Jerusalem. They sang the songs of Zion, and rejoiced when the towers of Jerusalem and the Golden Temple came into view, and as they came down the road over Olivet they probably made their camp there where they could look across the valley to the Temple. Everything was moving. Flocks of sheep and herds of oxen were being driven toward the Temple, and crowds of people from near and far were filling the streets, and also moving toward the Holy House.

When Jesus came into the Temple Court He saw something that stirred his whole soul with sorrow and wrath. The sellers of sheep, and oxen, and doves, and the money-changers had brought their things into the great court inside the marble pillars, and on the pavement of many-colored marbles, and were buying and selling noisily, and turning the courts of the Lord into a market. The voices of men and animals must have disturbed those who worshipped in the inner courts. The priests allowed it, perhaps they were paid for doing so, and Jesus, as a Son in His Father's house where the servants had been unfaithful, began clearing the court of all these things, and finding some cord on the pavement He folded it into a short scourge of many strands and used it to drive the cattle and sheep and their keepers out of court. The money-changers would not easily yield, but he poured out their money and overturned their tables, and to those who sold doves he said,

"Take these things hence; make not my Father's house a house of merchandise."

And the people wondered why they should obey this strange young man, but they did.

It was the Divine light in the face of Jesus, and not the bit of cord that drove them out. They saw that He had a right to clear the Temple courts.

Then the Jews wondered who had given Him this right, and they said to Him.

"What sign showest Thou unto us, seeing Thou doest these things?"

And this was the sign He gave them: "Destroy this Temple, and in three days I will raise it up."

He knew that they would not understand this, but they would remember it after they had crucified Him and He had risen from the dead, for He spoke of His body.

The Jews turned scornfully away. The Temple had been forty-six years in building, and they thought His promise an idle boast, but they did not forget it. Three years after they helped to bring Him to the cross, accusing Him in the High priests palace of saying these things.

CHAPTER XI.

A TALK ABOUT THE BREATH OF GOD.

Jesus was in the Temple most of the time during the Passover Feast. He taught the people standing among the marble pillars of the outer court. He also did miracles among them, and many believed on Him because of the miracles, but He, knowing their hearts, saw not one among them whom He would call to be with Him in His work, for He could not wholly trust them. The Pharisees and Doctors of the Law also stood and listened to Him, and among them was one whose heart turned toward Jesus. He was one of the highest of the Pharisees, but his heart was not so proud and full of self-love as the hearts of most of the Pharisees. His name was Nicodemus. He longed to talk with Jesus, but he was afraid of what the other Pharisees would say.

He found out where the camp of the Galilean company was, and one night went out of the city gate, across the Kedron bridge and up the slope of the Mount of Olives and found Jesus. There was no place to talk quietly in the crowded tents, so they must have gone out under the shadowy olive trees to talk.

"Master," he said—and it was much for the wise Pharisee to speak so humbly to the young carpenter of Galilee—"Master, we know that Thou art a teacher come from God, for no man can do these miracles that Thou doest except God be with him."

Jesus looked through the heart of Nicodemus, though it was night, and saw what he needed most, and so He made no reply about Himself or His miracles, but said,

"Verily, I say unto you, except a man be born again he cannot see the Kingdom of God."

Nicodemus could not understand how a man could be born when he is old, so Jesus explained that it was a spiritual birth. "That which is born of the flesh is flesh, and that which is born of the spirit is spirit." And as the wind softly stirred the leaves of the olive trees above their heads He said,

"The wind bloweth where it listeth, and thou hearest the sound thereof, but canst not tell whence it cometh and whither it bloweth. So is every one that is born of the Spirit."

Nicodemus had always thought that religion was the keeping of the law as all Jews were taught by the priests, so he was astonished, and said,

"How can these things be?"

"Art thou a master in Israel and knowest not these things?" said Jesus, and then He spoke to the soul of Nicodemus of the things of the Spirit of Heaven—The Heaven in which He already lived,—and of the new kingdom that had begun on earth.

If you will find what Jesus said to Nicodemus in the third chapter of John's Gospel you will find among other things these beautiful words,—

"For God so loved the world that he gave His only begotten Son, that whosoever believeth in Him should not perish, but have everlasting life."

Nicodemus found out that life was the breath of God in man, and that by it man lives. Perhaps he felt it within him as he went down the valley under the trees and heard the wind among the leaves; and as he came up the steep way and through the city gate in the silence of the night, perhaps he resolved to be a disciple of Jesus.

CHAPTER XII.

A TALK ABOUT THE WATER OF LIFE.

After the Passover there were many who had believed in Jesus who wished to be baptized, and so they went down to Jordan with Jesus and the disciples, and then the disciples baptized them.

John, who was also baptizing at another point by the river, was told that Jesus was baptizing and that all men were going to Him. John was rejoiced at this.

"This my joy therefore is fulfilled," he said. "He must increase, but I must decrease. He that cometh from heaven is above all."

After this Jesus went back to Galilee, and as He and His disciples went through the country of Samaria, which lay between Judea and Galilee, they came at noon near to the little village of Sychar among the hills. It was the most difficult road to Galilee, and most persons followed the Jordan road when going back and forth, for the Judeans and Samaritans were not friendly, but it is written that Jesus "must needs go through Samaria."

While the disciples went up into the village to buy some bread, Jesus sat down by a deep well in the valley. It was built round with stone, and covered from the sun, for the people prized the well not only for the clear, cold water, but because Jacob, the father of all the tribes of Israel dug the well for his family and cattle and flocks hundreds of years before.

While Jesus rested by the well a woman came down the path from the town to draw water. She drew the water with a strong cord that she fastened around her earthen water-jar and was going to put it on her shoulder and carry it away when Jesus asked her for a drink of water. She had not offered Him any for she thought a Jew would not ask even a drink of water from a Samaritan, but Jesus said,

"If thou knewest the gift of God, and who it is that saith to thee 'Give me to drink' thou wouldst have asked of Him and he would have given thee living water."

The woman did not understand His words about water any more than Nicodemus did about the blowing of the wind. Jesus was talking about *life* always and everwhere, but the people were slow to understand Him.

The woman wondered where Jesus could get better water than this from Jacob's well.

"Whosoever shall drink of this water," He said, "shall thirst again, but whosoever drinketh of the water that I shall give him shall never thirst. But the water that I shall give him shall be in him a well of water springing up into everlasting life."

When the woman heard this she asked for it, that she might not be thirsty and come to the well for water, but Jesus, seeing that she could not understand His words began to speak of her life, and so truly that she was amazed and said,

"Sir, I perceive that thou art a prophet." She talked of the mountain near by which had been the place of worship of the Samaritans, and of the Temple at Jerusalem where the Jews worshipped, for she did not want to talk of her own life, which was not good.

Jesus then showed her that "God is a Spirit, and they that worship Him must worship Him in spirit and in truth," and that the hour had come when He wished people to worship him so in every place.

"I know that Messias cometh, which is called Christ," she said.

"I that speak unto thee am He," He said. Then the woman left her water-jar and hurried away without a word to tell the people of the town.

While she was away His disciples came and begged Jesus to eat, but His spirit was filled with the thought of life, and he said,

"I have meat to eat that ye know not of."

And when they did not understand He said,

"My meat is to do the will of Him that sent me, and finish His work," and when he thought how great the work was that was before Him, it was as if the harvest-time of gathering the people into the kingdom had come.

As they looked out along the valley men were ploughing the fields to sow wheat.

"Say ye not there are four months," He said, "and then cometh harvest? Behold I say unto you, 'Lift up your eyes and look on the fields; for they are white already to harvest.'"

While He stayed two days in Sychar many believed on him there.

"Now we believe," they said to the woman, not because of thy saying for we have heard Him ourselves, and know that this is indeed the Christ, the Saviour of the world."

CHAPTER XIII.

JESUS IN THE SYNAGOGUE.

Jesus came back to Galilee through the Valley of Jenin and across the plain of Jezreel to Cana, where His disciple Nathanael lived, and where He had wrought His first miracle. While He was in Cana a nobleman who lived at Capernaum came riding into the little town in great haste to asked Jesus to come down and heal his son who was near death. To try him, Jesus said,

"Except ye see signs and wonders ye will not believe."

The nobleman would not stop to talk of this, but besought Jesus, saying, "Sir, come down ere my child die."

Jesus was glad to see his faith, and ready to meet it.

"Go thy way," He said, "thy son liveth," and the man went away believing what Jesus had said. On the way down to Capernaum by the Lake, some glad-faced servants came hastening to meet him.

"Thy son liveth!" They cried—the very words that Jesus had used. When he asked them when the boy had taken a turn for the better they said,

"Yesterday at the seventh hour the fever left him."

JESUS IN THE SYNAGOGUE.

Then the happy father knew that it was at the seventh hour—one o'clock —that Jesus had said, "Thy son liveth."

There was joy in the house of the nobleman when the father and mother and all the household gathered around the boy who had been healed, and talked of the wonderful power of Jesus in speaking the word of healing.

From Cana Jesus went to Nazareth. John the Baptist had been thrown into a gloomy prison down by the Dead Sea by Herod Antipas because he had rebuked the wickedness of that king, and Jesus knew that His own work was now fully begun, since the prophet, who had come to prepare His way, was laid aside.

While Jesus was at home with His mother and brothers and sisters He went one Sabbath to the village church or synagogue, as He had always done through His childhood and youth. Perhaps His brothers and some of His disciples were with Him, while His mother and sisters parted from Him and entered by another door, as was the Jewish custom. There were many there who hoped that the young carpenter, who had become a teacher, and as many believed, a prophet, would read from the Book of the Law.

After the singing, and the prayers, and the reciting of the creeds, the time came for the reading and teaching. The first lesson had been read, and the ruler of the synagogue took from the sacred place where it was kept another parchment roll, and coming down the steps he handed it to Jesus. It was the roll of Isaiah, and as Jesus went up to the reader's desk He opened and unrolled it until He came to these words,

"The spirit of the Lord is upon me, because he hath annointed me to preach the gospel to the poor; He hath sent me to heal the broken-hearted, to preach deliverance to the captives, and recovering of sight to the blind, to set at liberty them that are bruised, to preach the acceptable year of the Lord."

When he had finished he rolled the book again and handed it to the minister and sat down. It was the custom of those who were teachers of the people to sit down to teach, while the people all rose and stood until he had finished.

"This day," said Jesus "is this scripture fulfilled in your ears."

The people were looking and listening so earnestly that it was very still, and as Jesus told them simply that He was the very One whom Isaiah had spoken of seven hundred years before, that He had brought the good tidings, and had come to do the work the prophet had spoken of, they looked at each other in amazement. To be sure they had never heard such words of grace and wisdom, but how could this be true?

"Is not this Joseph's son?" they asked each other. Joseph had been their neighbor and Jesus had grown up among them and played with their children. They thought some evil thing had entered into Him disturbing His mind. But when He began to tell them that no prophet was accepted in his own country, and that the Lord was obliged to send them to strangers, as He sent Elijah and Elisha, they were angry with Him. Some of the men wished to teach Him a lesson, and they took Him by force to the edge of a cliff, for Nazareth was built high up among the hills, and were about to cast Him over among the limestone rocks below, but turning away from them, Jesus walked quietly down the hill to the path that led into the valley—and no one was able to lay a hand upon Him to harm Him. "He came unto His own, and His own received Him not," and He went away to preach the good tidings in other towns. The heart of Mary must have been full of sorrow when she saw her Son "despised and rejected of men" as Isaiah prophesied, but she hid her sorrow, and remembered the words of the Lord brought to her by the angel before her Son was born.

And so Jesus went down to Capernaum where he had friends and disciples, and afterward His mother and His brothers went to Him there, but Nazareth knew him no more.

It was about this time that it is supposed that Jesus went alone to a religious feast at Jerusalem, and while there cured a poor man who could not walk. He lay on his mat near a spring called Bethesda. It was covered by a roof, and had five porches. Here the sick were brought by their friends that they might, when they saw the waters bubble up, step in and be cured. They believed then an angel came down and made the moving of the waters, but it was probably one of the kind called intermittent springs. There is one at Jerusalem now called the "Fountain of the Virgin" which rises at certain times.

Jesus saw the poor friendless man who had waited for thirty-eight years for the chance of stepping into the waters when they were moving, and had been disappointed for others stepped in before him. Looking at him, He said,

"Wilt thou be made whole?"

The man explained why he could not be cured, for there was no man to help him. Then Jesus said,

"Rise, take up thy bed, and walk."

He rose at once, and walked, carrying the mat on which he lay.

The Jews were angry when they heard of it for the man had been cured on the Sabbath, but Jesus told them that they were all refusing eternal life because of their unbelief, saying,

"Ye will not come unto Me that yet might have life."

CHAPTER XIV.

AMONG THE FISHERMEN.

Capernaum was on the shore of the beautiful lake of Galilee. There were villages clustered around the lake then and all Galilee was swarming with busy life, but now there are few inhabitants, and Capernaum is only a heap of stones. Some of these stones, which may now be seen, are carved in such a way that we may know that they are a part of an ancient synagogue. This was the synagogue, perhaps, that a good Centurion built whose servant Jesus cured when he was near death, and here in Capernaum lived the nobleman whose son Jesus cured by a word, and here lived His first disciples, Peter and Andrew, and James and John, and here Matthew, who sat in his little office taking the taxes that the people had to pay, may have seen Jesus pass, and may have heard him speak before he became a disciple.

The beautiful plain of Gennesaret spreads out from one end of the lake, and there is a white beach of shells there, while at other points on the lake there are hills and great rocks close to the water.

On this white beach Jesus stood one spring morning teaching the people. As the fisher-folks and others gathered close around to hear Him, He was pushed so near the water that He stepped into Peter's boat, which was near the shore, and asked him to push it out a little way into the water, and there in the stern of the boat Jesus sat and taught the people who stood thick upon the shore.

The boat of Zebedee, the father of James and John was near by, for they were the partners of Peter and Andrew. They had washed their nets and had given up fishing until night again, for morning was not a good time for fishing, but Jesus said to Peter and Andrew,—

"Launch out into the deep, and let down your nets for a draught."

The disciples were surprised at this, for it was not the hour for fishing, and Peter said,

"Master, we have toiled all night and have taken nothing; nevertheless at thy word I will let down the net."

When they had done this they found that their nets were filled with fishes, so that they called to James and John to come and help them, for their nets were breaking. When they had emptied the nets into the two boats they were filled so full that they began to sink.

Then Peter fell down at Jesus's knees and cried out,—

"Depart from me, for I am a sinful man, O Lord!" so wonderful did the miracle seem to him.

But to Peter Jesus said,—

"Fear not; from henceforth thou shalt catch men." James and John He also called, and showed them that the time had now come for them to help Him in founding the Kingdom.

They did not wait to sell the great draught of fishes that they had brought to land; and they did not wait to sell their fishing boats and nets, but they forsook all and followed Jesus. They did not know that their names would be known forever as the founders of the Christian Church with Him who was its divine Head.

CHAPTER XV.

THE HEALING HAND OF JESUS.

The Jewish church, or synagogue at Capernaum was very beautiful. It was of white marble, and richly carved, and was the gift of a Roman officer to the Jews.

One Sabbath morning Jesus went in and sat among the learned Rabbis, for He wished to speak to the people as He had near Nazareth. The people knew and loved him, and the place was crowded to hear Him speak. He sat there through the singing, and the prayers, and the reading.

The parchment rolls of the law and the prophets were in a case behind Him; and there was the curtain, and the branched candlesticks. Then He went to the Teacher's seat, and while all the people stood He sat and taught them. People wondered, as they always did, at his words, for they were not like the words of the Rabbis,—they were as if God Himself were speaking through a man.

In the midst of it there was a loud cry from a man who looked like a maniac. He had followed the people in, and the words of Jesus had disturbed the evil spirit that was in Him.

"Let us alone," it cried, "what have we to do with thee, thou Jesus of Nazareth. Art thou come to destroy us? I know thee who Thou art,—the Holy One of God."

"Hold thy peace, and come out of Him," said Jesus, and the poor man fell headlong on the marble floor, but in a moment he was free, for the evil spirit had obeyed the word of Jesus, and this astonished the people so much that they told it through all the town and the country round about.

When He went home from the synagogue, for Peter's house was one of His homes, He found the mother of Peter's wife very ill of fever, and they brought Jesus to her bed. He bent over her and said some words to that which had caused the fever, and at once it was gone.

She seemed to be quite well again, and her first wish was to do something for this wonderful man whom Peter had been following, and she rose and helped to prepare food for Him.

The people did not dare to come to Jesus for healing while it was yet the Sabbath, for the Rabbis said it was wrong to cure people on the Sabbath day, but as soon as the sun had set the Sabbath ended, and then the streets were filled with people who came for themselves, or bringing their sick friends to be touched by the hand of Jesus. All around the little house of Peter they crowded, while He walked among them looking at them with pitying love, and "He laid his hands on every one of them, and healed them."

CHAPTER XVI.

FOLLOWING JESUS.

The next morning Jesus went out among the hills alone. All day He was pressed upon by the poor, the sick, the blind, and the lame, or those who were hungry for the word, and so at night or early morning He went out to be alone, to think of the great work he had come to do, and to pray or talk to the Father, for Jesus and the Father were one. But the people followed Him, and begged him not to leave them.

THE NET FULL OF FISHES.

"I must preach the kingdom of God to other cities also," He said, "for therefore am I sent." And He took his disciples and started on a journey from village to village through Galilee. There were about two hundred of these towns, and they were near together. It was the springtime, and the fields and hills between the villages were beautiful with flowers and growing grain. Sometimes He taught in their churches, and sometimes under their trees or trellises, and wherever He went the common people heard him gladly.

Once as He drew near a town a leper followed Him. He followed Him into the town, which was against the law, for the leper was not allowed to live inside a town, or to come near the people, as the touch of a leper would give the disease to another. But so earnest was he to see Jesus that he came through the crowd and fell on his face before Jesus, saying,

"Lord if Thou wilt, Thou canst make me clean."

Jesus put forth His hand and touched him, saying, "I will; be thou clean."

Suddenly the leprosy left the man, and his dead and filthy skin became as healthy as a child's, and Jesus sent him to the priest to offer that which the law commanded for the cleansing of lepers. It was a long, and often costly process that a leper must pass through to be cleansed from his disease, but the word of Jesus was with power, and brought divine life to take the place of death, for leprosy was a slow death.

When the Lord came back to Capernaum the people thronged Him, and when He rested in the shaded court of a friend's house it was soon filled with the eager people who longed to hear His word, or be healed by His touch.

Once it was so crowded in the court that some men, who were bringing a friend to Jesus who was helpless with palsy, took him up by the outside stairs to the housetop. There, by taking up a few tiles, they made an opening just over the place where Jesus sat, and the people soon saw the man lying on his mat before Jesus, for they had let it down by cords through the opening.

Jesus saw the faith of the four men who had let their sick friend down at His feet, and it touched His heart. He also saw the longing in the soul of the sick man to be good and pure, and He said,

"Son, be of good cheer, thy sins be forgiven thee."

The Scribes, who were always copying the Scriptures—for there was no printing done in those days—were always watching to hear Jesus say something contrary to the Law of Moses, that they might tell it to the priests,

JESUS HEALING THE SICK.

and some who were sitting there looked at each other and said in their hearts,

"Who can forgive sins but God only?"

Jesus heard their thoughts and asked them why they reasoned in this way with themselves, and which seemed to them the easier, to forgive sins or to heal the body.

But that they might know that He had power over the body as well as the soul He said to the sick man,

"Arise; take up thy bed, and go thy way into thine house."

The man rose and rolled up his mat and carried it out, the people falling back astonished to let him pass, for his palsy had left him and he walked out strong and well.

"We have seen strange things to-day," the people said among themselves for they could not understand how a man could forgive sins or heal disease.

When Jesus left the house to go down to the sea-shore He passed the Custom-house, where the tax-gatherers, or "publicans," gathered money from the Jewish people to pay to their conquerors, the Romans.

The Romans were very hard in their dealings with the Jews, and made themselves rich by taking money from the poor of their provinces.

The people did not like the tax-gatherer, and his was not a pleasant office.

Levi, also called Matthew, was a rich tax-gatherer at Capernaum, and as he sat in his office looking out upon the market-place he saw Jesus passing by. Perhaps he had often heard Jesus teach by the shore and in the market-place, and longed to follow Him. He saw the Teacher stop at his open door, and heard Him say,

"Follow Me."

That was enough; Matthew left all, rose up and followed Jesus. He had a business that made him rich, but he was ready to leave it all to be a disciple of Jesus.

He wanted all to know that he had chosen a new life, and so he gave a great dinner to his friends, and invited Jesus and His five disciples that he might confess before them all his faith in Jesus.

The Pharisees looked down upon the publicans and thought them a people unfit to associate with, and when they passed by and saw Jesus sitting in Matthew's house at the feast they asked His disciples as they went in and out why their Master ate with "publicans and sinners," a thing they felt themselves too good to do.

Jesus Himself answered them in words that have helped many sinful people to come to Him since.

"They that are whole need not a physician, but they that are sick. I came not to call the righteous but sinners to repentance."

And then He turned to talk with Matthew and his friends, who listened to every word that fell from His lips, and did not try to find fault with Him as the Pharisees did.

Matthew had made a rich feast, and his table was no doubt piled with the beautiful fruits of the plain of Gennesaret, but the eyes of all and the thoughts of all were fixed upon the wonderful Teacher, and Matthew, the publican, who had become His disciple.

CHAPTER XVII.

FRIENDS OF JESUS.

Jesus had a good and true reason for choosing just twelve men to help Him to begin to build the first Christian Church, or the Kingdom of Heaven on the earth. We cannot yet understand the reason for everything He did, but quite enough to help us to believe in Him, and to give us a place in His kingdom. He had called half that number and soon He called six more to join them, and named them apostles.

Before He called them He went up into a mountain to be alone. He left Capernaum and went up through a rocky vale to a high plain where the grass lay thick and the wild flowers were coming up among it, for it was spring-time. Two hills, or peaks rose out of this plain, and there was a grassy hollow between. They were called the "Horns of Hattin." From one of these hills Jesus could see the lake with its cities, and the plain dotted with villages below, and beyond them the great Mount Hermon crowned with snow. Here Jesus stayed all night, and the next morning came down into the grassy dale between the peaks where the people were gathering. The disciples went to meet Him, and He told them that He had chosen twelve of them to be with Him in His work, and to preach the Good Tidings to the people.

He called to His side Peter and Andrew, and James and John—the two pairs of brothers who were His first friends; then Philip, of Bethsaida, Bartholomew, from Cana, and Matthew, the tax-gatherer of Capernaum, who afterward wrote the first gospel. He also chose Thomas, of Galilee; James and Jude, two brothers from Capernaum; Simon, of Galilee, and Judas Iscariot, who came from the country near Jerusalem. Five of these, it is said, were His cousins. More than half of them were fisherman, and none of them were learned men, unless Bartholomew might be called one. How wonderful it must have been to see these twelve earnest young men gathered around Jesus, ready to go where He should send them, or follow Him to death. No kings or emperors on earth ever had so great honor given them as that which Jesus gave to these men, for they became the Lord's spiritual brothers, and princes in His spiritual kingdom.

Then Jesus came down among the people. Some had brought sick friends up the rocky gorge for Jesus to touch; or they had brought poor souls possessed by devils for Him to set free, and He healed them all.

Then He sat down and taught the people. The sayings of that wonderful day are kept in the gospels, and are called the "Sermon on the Mount." There was no choir, no organ, no church made with hands, but the words are now read in every Christian church in the world. The preacher sat on a green hillock, His dark cloak thrown back showing His white tunic, and the spring sunshine lay on His holy, beautiful face and flowing hair. All this the people saw, but they saw much more than this. They saw something divine in His face, His form, and the light around Him, and what they heard seemed to them to be the words of a Divine Man. He looked lovingly on the little group of disciples near Him, and blessed them in beautiful words that we call the Beatitudes, or the Ten Blessings. He said to them and to us that the "blessed" (happy) are the good, humble, pure souls who have little of this world's wealth and friendship, but much faith and love.

If you will read the fifth, sixth and seventh chapters of Matthew you will know much that Jesus taught that heavenly day on Hattin Mount. He taught them the law of love and forgiveness; the law of purity and truth. He taught them to be humble and simple, especially in prayer, and not like the Pharisees. He gave them a wonderful prayer that we call "the Lord's Prayer," though it is a prayer to the Lord, for all Christians in all ages to bring to Him. He told them that if they were children of God they could not be worldly, loving themselves and the world best; neither could they serve two masters. Then He taught them a beautiful lesson of trust in the Heavenly Father by pointing to the birds that flew above them, and reminding them how they were fed and cared for; and also by pointing to the wild field lilies that grew near by, their scarlet petals shining in the sun.

SERMON ON THE MOUNT.

"Consider the lilies of the field how they grow," he said, "they toil not, neither do they spin, and yet I say unto you that even Solomon in all his glory was not arrayed like one of these," and then He asked them if God, who clothed the lilies, would not clothe His own children, and told them to have no fear for the future, but to seek the Kingdom of God first and always, and all needed things would be given to them.

Then He looked away from the birds and the lilies into the eyes of the people and saw their need of love and truth, for he could read their hearts. He told them that they should not judge each other, or look long upon each other's faults, but rather upon their own, and showed them how they might ask God for love and truth, and it would surely be given them, because the Heavenly Father is more just, and kind, and loving than an earthly father can be.

And here is the Golden Rule of Christ, which, if we live by it, will bring heaven down to earth.

"Whatsoever ye would that men should do to you, do ye even so to them."

He told them that the way of the world was wide, and many were crowding into it, while the heavenly way was narrow in this life, and few were finding it, though many talked much about it, and seemed to have found it. He said that it would be shown in the day when we all appear before God who has truly followed Him. He said that the true men were like the wise man who built his house upon a rock, and when the winds, the rain, and the flood came it stood fast, because it was founded on the rock; and the false were like the foolish man who built his house upon the sand, and when the winds, and the rain, and the floods came it fell, and great was the fall of it.

The people went away from this great meeting among the hills to think it over. It was so new and so wonderful, not at all like the teaching of the scribes, for the young carpenter of Nazareth spoke like a Teacher of teachers. Ever since that day when the Lord sat and taught the truths of the Kingdom of Heaven, and the people stood upon the grassy plain among the spring flowers and the wild thyme to hear his words, the Sermon on the Mount has been known as the greatest sermon the world has ever known.

CHAPTER XVIII.

THE LORD OF LIFE.

Jesus came down to Capernaum again and found the same crowds of needy people, who were like sheep having no shepherd. The rich as well as the poor had their wants and their troubles.

A good Roman officer, called a Centurion, because he was captain over a hundred men, had a servant who was so faithful to him that he was very fond of him. The servant was very sick, and when the Centurion heard that Jesus was again in Capernaum he went to the chief men of the city and asked them to get Jesus to come and cure his servant. He feared to ask the favor himself, for he thought Jesus was a Jew who would not like to have dealings with the Romans. So the Jews spoke to Jesus about it saying that the Centurion was the good man who had built a beautiful synagogue for them. Jesus did not need to be urged to be kind to a Roman for He loved all the people of the earth alike.

While He was on His way some friends of the Centurion came to meet Him with a message.

"Lord, trouble not Thyself," he said, "for I am not worthy that Thou shouldst enter under my roof: Wherefore neither thought I myself worthy to come unto Thee; but say in a word and my servant shall be healed."

Jesus told the people who followed Him that He had not found such faith as this among their own people. And when the men returned to the Centurion's house they found the servant cured of his sickness.

But some of the Jews were offended because Jesus had said that a pagan Roman could have more faith than a Jew, and that they would enter the Kingdom of Heaven while the Jews would be left out.

The next day Jesus and His disciples went to a little city called Nain, set up among the hills, more than twenty miles away. When they were near the city gate they met a funeral procession coming out. They were going to the burying ground on a hillside not far away. There were hired mourners, as is the custom in that country, who made many doleful noises, and behind them came a weeping woman—the mother of the young man who had died.

His body was borne by friends and followed by many more, for all felt sorry for the poor woman who had lost her only son.

As the procession passed Jesus said two little words to the woman—"Weep not," and then He put forth His hand and touched the bier. The men who bore it set it down before Jesus who looked down into the face of the dead, saying,

"Young man, I say unto thee, arise!"

In a moment the young man opened his eyes, sat up, and began to speak, and Jesus gave him back from the grave to his happy mother.

While Jesus was near Nain some of the disciples of John the Baptist came to see Him. John was in prison still, down in the low, hot country by the Dead Sea. He had heard strange stories about Jesus from the disciples who came to see him, and because they were not settled in their mind about Him, John sent them to find Him and to say,

"Art thou He that should come, or do we look for another?"

Jesus told them to go and tell John what they saw.

"The blind receive their sight and the lame walk, the lepers are cleansed, and the deaf hear, the dead are raised up, and the poor have the gospel preached to them, and blessed is he whosoever shall not be offended in me."

Then Jesus taught the people who stood by, and the lesson ended with these words which he speaks to the whole world,

"Come unto me, all ye that labor and are heavy laden, and I will give you rest; take my yoke upon you and learn of me, for I am meek and lowly of heart, and ye shall find rest unto your souls; for my yoke is easy and my burden is light."

This is the loving invitation of Jesus to every one of us to enter the Kingdom of Heaven, and it is the King Himself who invites us.

CHAPTER XIX.

MARY OF MAGDALA.

There was a Pharisee named Simon, who was very curious to know what Jesus taught, although he had no wish to be His disciple. He was a rich man and lived in a beautiful house with a court. Beyond the court was a banqueting room with couches on which guests sat leaning upon the tables in the Eastern fashion. There were other guests invited to hear Jesus talk, the friends of

Simon, and it is quite probable that when they came the servants of Simon met them and took their sandals and washed their feet and arranged their hair as was the custom, and were also heartily welcomed by Simon. When Jesus came He had no such service or welcome given Him, for Simon did not love Him; he was only curious about Him.

While they were at the tables a beautiful young woman came in through the open door and passed swiftly by the couches on which the guests were reclining until she came to the place where Jesus was. No one spoke to her or about her, for they all knew that she had been a sinful woman. But soon they saw that she bent weeping over the feet of Jesus where He lay upon the couch, and soon they knew by the odor of costly perfume that she was anointing His feet. As her tears fell she wiped His feet with her long hair, and kissed them again and again.

Simon looked at her severely, but said nothing, though he wondered in his heart why Jesus did not know that a sinful woman was touching Him. Then said Jesus,

"Simon, I have somewhat to say to thee." And Simon replied, "Master, say on."

Then Jesus told a little story of a man who had two debtors; one owed him five hundred pence, and the other fifty; and when they had nothing to pay he frankly forgave them both. Then he asked which of them will love Him most?"

"I suppose that he to whom he forgave most," said Simon, and Jesus told him that he was right.

Then He turned and pointed to the woman, saying,

"See'st thou this woman?" and the eyes of all were fixed on the weeping Mary of Magdala.

When Jesus had told Simon that he had failed to bring water for His feet, though she had washed them with her tears, and wiped them with her hair; that he had given Him no kiss of welcome, and she had not ceased to kiss His feet; that he had not anointed His head with oil, but she had anointed His feet with costly ointment, He added,

"Her sins which are many are forgiven; for she loved much; but to whom little is forgiven the same loveth little." And turning to the woman He said,

"Thy sins are forgiven; thy faith hath saved thee; go in peace."

As Jesus went through the villages of Galilee He found many friends and many enemies. The twelve were with Him, learning daily the wonderful lessons He taught, and preparing to be preachers of the glad tidings also.

Not only Mary of Magdala, but Susanna, and Joanna, the wife of King Herod's steward who had been cured by Him, were His grateful friends. Some priests came down from Jerusalem to watch Him, and to tell the people that He was not a true teacher, and this pleased the Pharisees. They saw that He did wonderful things that no man could do, but they said that He did it by the power of the spirit of evil, and they asked Him to show them a sign that he was from God.

The Lord spoke words to the Pharisees that must have burned like coals of fire, for it showed how false and wicked their hearts were while their outward life seemed to be very religious.

He told them that no sign should be given them except that of Jonah; as he was three days and three nights in the great fish, so should the Son of Man be three days and three nights in the heart of the earth, and though the men of Nineveh were wicked, yet they repented at the preaching of Jonah, but the men of Jerusalem did not repent, though a greater than Jonah was among them.

Mary and her sons had come from Nazareth hoping to take Jesus away from the crowds, perhaps, for a rest among the hills, for the summer heat was great down by the lake and along the Jordan. Some one sent word to Jesus, as He sat teaching within the court of a house, that His mother and brothers were outside, and wished to speak with Him. The crowd was too great for them to enter. Before Jesus rose to go out to his mother, He paused a moment to teach the great lesson He had come to bring to the world. Looking at His disciples He said,

"My mother and my brethren are these which hear the Word of God and do it."

CHAPTER XX.

STORIES TOLD BY THE LAKE.

Jesus was glad to go among the fishermen and teach the people by the Lake, for their hearts were like the good ground into which the farmer loves to drop his seed, while the hearts of the rich, proud Pharisees were like the rock on which seed cannot grow. Perhaps he was thinking of this as He walked out one morning from Peter's house along the pebbly shore and sat down to talk with the people. The crowd always grew large around him there, and He had to again enter a fishing boat and sit a little out from the shore that the people might see and hear Him more easily. He taught them as no man had ever done before. He told them short stories, often taking the subject from something the people could see. Perhaps this morning as He looked over the lovely plain of Gennesaret, He saw a sower casting seed into a brown and furrowed field, for it was the time of the year for sowing the winter wheat. This is the story of "The Sower:"

"A sower went out to sow his seed," said Jesus, "and as he sowed, some fell by the wayside, and it was trodden down, and the fowls of the air devoured it.

"And some fell upon a rock; and as soon as it was sprung up it withered away, because it lacked moisture.

"And some fell among thorns, and the thorns sprang up with it and choked it.

"And other fell on good ground, and sprang up and bore fruit an hundred fold."

And then He said, "He that hath ears to hear let him hear," for He knew that some could understand with the heart that He was talking of the Word of God, but there were many who could not.

His disciples asked Him to make the story plain to all, and so He said,

"The seed is the Word of God. Those by the wayside are they that hear; then cometh the devil and taketh away the Word out of their hearts lest they should believe and be saved.

"They on the rock are they which, when they hear, receive the Word with joy, and these have no root, which for a while believe, and in time of temptation fall away.

"And that which fell among thorns are they which, when they have heard, go forth, and are choked with cares and riches and pleasures of this life, and bring no fruit to perfection.

"But that on the good ground are they which in an honest and good heart, having heard the Word, keep it, and bring forth fruit with patience."

He also told them a story called "The Wheat and the Tares," of a man who sowed good seed in a field, but when it sprung up and bore grain there were weeds growing among it called tares, for an enemy had sowed the seed at night and it had grown up with the wheat. The man's servants wished to pull out the tares, but the master of the field said both should grow together

JESUS TEACHING BY THE SEA.

until the harvest, that the wheat might not be uprooted with the tares. At the end of the harvest the tares would be burned and the wheat gathered into the barn. In this way he taught them why good and evil are allowed to grow together in this world.

He also taught them in the story of "The Mustard Seed," that the growth of the Lord's Kingdom in the heart is like a mustard seed sowed in a field—which is the least of seeds—but which becomes a great plant, so large that birds light on its branches. He told them other stories also that were to show them that the Kingdom of Heaven was life, and not a written law, and that it grows in the hearts of people as a seed grows in a field, one seed bearing many seeds, until the time when the Lord's Kingdom shall fill the earth as the ripe wheat fills the field in harvest.

One of the stories told that day was about "The Treasure." He told them of a man who, when digging in a field, found a treasure, a mine of gold, perhaps, and went and sold all that he had to get money enough to buy that field. Another one was the story of "The Pearl," which a pearl-hunter found. It was so large and beautiful that he sold all he had to be able to buy it. Both these stories were to teach that heaven in the heart is worth more to us, when once we find it, than all the treasures or pleasures of this world.

He also told a story of a "Fishing Net," which caught fish of every kind, but when it was drawn to shore the fishermen gathered the good fish into baskets, but threw the bad away. This story was something like that of the "Wheat and the Tares," showing how good and evil are at last separated.

This was a wonderful day by the blue waters of the Lake of Galilee. The people went home thinking much about the new Teacher and His stories of the Kingdom of Heaven.

The great Sower of the Seed had been dropping it into their hearts, and He alone knew which hearts were "good ground."

CHAPTER XXI.

STILLING THE STORMS.

When Jesus was very tired from teaching the people and healing the sick He used to cross the lake and go up among the rocks of Gadara, a wild region where there were few villages. After the last long day of teaching

STILLING THE STORMS.

by the shore Jesus needed rest, but neither at Peter's house, nor anywhere on that side of the Lake could He get away from the crowds that followed Him to hear Him, or to be healed by Him.

In the evening, when the people came back to Him, He took the large fishing-boat with His disciples, and set out for the other side. Several beside His disciples wished to go with Him. A scribe wished to follow Him, but Jesus told him that He had no home, no place to lay his head, though the foxes had holes and the birds of the air had nests. Perhaps Jesus saw that the scribe was not ready to leave all and follow Him. Another wished to go, but thought he ought first to bury his father, but Jesus said to him,

"Follow me, and let the dead bury their dead." This He said of the Jews who were spiritually dead.

After they had gone far out upon the Lake a great wind storm rose. It came sweeping down upon them from the hills, rattling the ropes and swelling the sails so that they had to bring them down and fasten them, and and then take the oars. Every part of the little ship was covered with spray from the rising waves, and the disciples began to feel afraid.

Where was Jesus? He was asleep. They had brought a cushion for His head, and He had fallen asleep in the stern of the ship. As a wave fell upon them and they were in danger of sinking they woke Jesus saying,

"Master, Master, we perish!"

Then He rose and spoke to the winds and waters, and the storm ceased, and there was a great calm.

The fishermen had never seen anything so wonderful as this, and they looked at each other, almost more afraid of Jesus than they had been of the storm.

"What manner of man is this," they said, "that even the wind and the sea obey Him!"

Jesus also wondered, and said,

"Why are ye so fearful? How is it that ye have no faith?"

As soon as they had landed in Gadara a strange man came out of the rock tombs to meet them. He was naked and wounded, for he was always wandering in the mountains and among the tombs, crying and cutting himself. Jesus was sorry for him for He knew that it was the evil spirits within him that made him so unhappy. The poor man tried to worship Jesus, and the evil spirits only cried out the more, begging to be let alone.

When Jesus asked "What is thy name," he answered, "My name is Legion, for we are many."

Jesus made the poor man free by commanding the evil spirits to come out of him. They entered into a herd of swine near by, and the frightened creatures ran down a steep place into the lake and were drowned. The men who kept them were afraid and ran away, telling all whom they met of the thing that had happened. Some people came to see for themselves, and they found the wild man of the tombs clothed and quietly sitting at the feet of Jesus listening to His word. They were afraid of Jesus and begged Him to go away. They did not understand that He wished to bless and not to harm them.

As He went back to the ship the man who had been cured of his insanity begged to go with Him, but Jesus told him to go instead to his friends at home and tell them what the Lord had done for him.

The next morning the people of Decapolis heard a strange story from the wild man of the tombs, but was now a reasoning man again.

And so Jesus stilled the storm of wind on the Lake and the storm of evil in a soul.

CHAPTER XXII.

CALLED BACK.

When Jesus came back to Capernaum He found the crowd of friends at the little wharf full of concern about Him, and glad that no harm had come to Him during the storm. Among them was one who had watched anxiously for the boat, for he had a little daughter at home very ill indeed, so ill that she was "at the last breath." His name was Jairus, and he was a ruler of the synagogue. He was so troubled that he fell at the feet of Jesus, begging Him to come and lay His hand on his child that she might live.

Jeuss went with him, a throng of people with them, hoping to see Him do a great work.

While He was on the way a woman who had been sick twelve years followed close behind Him, and put forth her hand timidly toward Him.

"If I may touch but His clothes I shall be whole," she said to herself, and she touched them with faith in her heart.

Jesus, who knew all hearts, turned straight around and said:

"Who touched My clothes?"

THE LITTLE GIRL, WHO WAS CALLED BACK.

How the woman shrank back and trembled when she heard that, for she was afraid she had done wrong.

The disciples thought it strange that He should ask this, as the people thronged so close that they could not help touching Jesus. But the woman knew what He meant and she came and fell down before Him, fearing and trembling, and told Him all the truth.

Jesus did not look sternly at her as she thought He would do, but He said gently,

"Daughter, thy faith hath made thee whole; go in peace, and be whole of thy plague."

While the woman was still at His feet full of gratitude and love because she felt herself cured, some friends came from the ruler's house to bring sad news.

"Thy daughter is dead," they said, "why troublest thou the Master any further?"

Jesus saw the looks of grief on the father's face and said quickly,

"Be not afraid, only believe."

So they went to the ruler's house, and into the inner room where the little maid lay. Many wished to press in after them to see what Jesus would do, but he took only Peter and James and John with the father and mother of the maiden into the quiet, darkened room. As He went in He said to some who were mourning noisily in the outer room,

"Weep not; she is not dead, but sleepeth." Jesus loved to call death a "sleep," for He knew that we never die. Then He took the little maid by the hand and called her. She had not gone so far into the country we cannot see that she could not hear a divine Voice calling to her,

"*Talitha cumi!*" ("Maiden, arise!") At once she rose and walked. She was a little girl of twelve, and very dear to her father and mother, and there was no doubt great joy as well as wonder in the house of the ruler that bright morning after the storm. In their joy and wonder there was danger of forgetting to give her the food she was in need of, and so Jesus gently reminded them, commanding that something should be given her to eat, but he charged them not to talk about the return of their little daughter.

CHAPTER XXIII.

TWO BY TWO.

Jesus had a desire to once more speak to the people of His own little town of Nazareth, and so He came again to His own, but His own received Him not. Once more he went into the Nazareth Synagogue where He had listened to the reading of the law all through His childhood, and to teach as He had done nine or ten months before. They did not rise up and thrust Him out as they did then, but they cast cold looks and scornful words upon Him. They could not understand His great power and wisdom, but they would not believe in Him.

"Is not this the carpenter, the Son of Mary," they said, "the brother of James and Joses, and of Juda and Simon? And are not His sisters here with us?" They were offended with Him. Jesus, knowing their faults said,

"A prophet is not without honor, but in his own country, and among his own kin, and in his own house."

He wondered why they were so unbelieving, when in His great love for them He was ready to do works of mercy among them, and to tell them the glad tidings of the Kingdom of Heaven, but He laid His hands on a few sick folk and healed them, and that was all.

As He went away to come back no more, His heart turned toward the many who were waiting for the tidings that His old friends had rejected, and He called the twelve together to send them out, two by two, into the world around them. He gave them power to cast out evil spirits, and to heal the sick; and He put the preaching power within them so that they could tell to others the wonderful truths of the Kingdom of Heaven. He told them that they must take nothing for their journey, except a staff, with which to walk over the steep mountain paths. He told them also to bless the house that sheltered them, and to leave the house or the city that would not receive them. He said that they would have many trials, and that their lives would be sought by wicked men, but that they need not fear, for the very hairs of their head were numbered, and that even a sparrow could not fall to the ground without their Father, and they were of more value than many sparrows.

He said many other words to them that gave them comfort and strength. They had left all to follow Him, and He showed them how, in losing their all in this life they were finding much more than that—even eternal life.

So, two by two, they went forth and left Jesus alone.

That great and good man, John the Baptist, was still in the prison of King Herold Antipas, down by the Dead Sea. He had been there more than a year, but no word came from the king saying that he was free. Queen Herodias wanted him to be put to death for he had spoken against her marriage with King Herod. She was a wicked woman, and the evil hate the good. Herod believed in his heart that John should go free, but for the Queen's sake he kept him in prison, but allowed his friends to see him, and sometimes sent for him secretly to hear him talk of the Kingdom of Heaven.

On the king's birthday he gave a great feast to his lords and captains, and when they had been served with dainty food in dishes of silver and gold, and had tasted the rare fruits and the costly wines, the dancing girls came in to flit over the polished marble floor, and wave their airy scarfs to please the king and his guests.

At last a young girl came in and danced alone. She was dressed like a princess, and she was a princess.

Queen Herodias had sent her young daughter, Salome, where an innocent girl and a queen's daughter should not have gone.

She pleased the king and his lords greatly, and when she had finished, and had knelt before the king to hear what he had to say to her, he cried,

"Ask of me whatsoever thou wilt, and I will give it thee," and with an oath he declared that he would certainly do it if she should ask the half of his kingdom.

She did not decide for herself, but ran to her mother, saying,

"What shall I ask?" And the cruel mother said,

"The head of John the Baptist."

King Herod did not expect this. He thought she might ask for some jewel of great price, or perhaps a royal palace for her very own, and when he heard her request he was very sorry. But an oath made before his lords could not be broken.

He sent men to the prison, and the good prophet, who had never known fear, went home to God, and they brought his head to the princess who gave it to her mother. The king's feast ended in gloom, and the poor girl, who only obeyed her wicked mother, had nothing but a dreadful memory to keep forever as the king's gift.

And the king himself—what trouble followed him during the rest of his life! Riches and honors were all taken from him, and he was sent out of his own country, while John had gone to his Father's house in the Heavenly Country to suffer no more forever.

John's disciples buried the body of their beloved master, and then went and told Jesus. Only Jesus can give real comfort in trouble.

The disciples—now called apostles, or teachers—who had been out teaching among the villages, heard, perhaps, of the death of John the Baptist, and came back to Jesus two by two, as they had gone out. They had been preaching, healing the sick, and casting out evil spirits. They often said "The Kingdom of Heaven is at hand," and the people wondered if it would not be best to rise up and make Jesus their king.

Herod heard of the work of Jesus and the apostles, and was afraid. He half believed that John whom he had killed had risen from the dead. He tried to see Jesus, but the One who had come to preach the gospel to the poor had no time to give to Herod.

As Peter, and John, and Andrew and all the rest came back they were full of stories of the wonderful things that had been done through the power that the Lord had given them. Many came with them to find Jesus. He saw that they needed to come away from the crowds that were always around them so that He could speak to them of their work, and so that they could rest, and think, and pray.

They took a boat and crossed the Lake. The shore was crowded with people who wished to be with Jesus, and when they knew that He was going to Bethsaida-Julias at the northern end of the Lake they resolved to follow Him, for it was only a few miles away.

At the end of the Lake they entered the Jordan river, and sailing up a little way to the landing-place they saw the people coming, some in boats, and more in groups along the shore—men, women and children—and Jesus, filled with love and pity for them, led them to a green hillside where He sat down to teach them as He had often done before.

It was spring, and the grass was like a great green carpet sprinkled with bright wild-flowers, while the river, lined with bushes flowed below, and beyond lay the beautiful blue Lake. The disciples stood around their Master while He taught the people in simple language that they could understand the greatest truths the world has ever heard. All the afternoon He spoke to them, and when the sun was slowly going down over the hills of Galilee they still wished to stay. They were as sheep having no shepherd. The disciples were troubled about them, for they were far from the villages where bread could be bought, and they had nothing to eat. They begged Jesus to send them away.

"Give ye them to eat," said Jesus. Then the disciples were astonished, for there were about five thousand men, beside the women and children. "Shall we go and buy two hundred pennyworth of bread, and give them to eat?" said Philip. Then Jesus, who knew what He would do, said, "How many loaves have ye? Go and see."

They went among the people, and Andrew came back, saying,

"There is a lad here which hath five barley loaves, and two small fishes; but what are they among so many?"

Then Jesus told His disciples to seat all the people in order upon the green grass, and soon there were little companies of fifty, and larger ones of an hundred sitting all over the hillside with their faces turned toward Jesus, who stood looking out upon them as a father would look upon his children. What were they waiting for? No one knew, but they saw Him take the little lad's basket of bread and the two little fishes and look up to heaven, blessing them as He did so. Then He began to break the bread and divide the fishes. As He broke the bread and gave to the disciples they took it away to the people sitting on the grass, and when they came back to Jesus there was still more waiting for them. In this way all the people were fed.

When they were satisfied Jesus said to His disciples.

"Gather up the fragments that remain, that nothing be lost."

And they filled twelve baskets with the pieces of the barley loaves that were left.

What a silent and wonderful supper of bread fresh from the hand of its Creator!

At last they began saying to each other in a low voice,

"This is of a truth that Prophet that should come into the world!" and they began to ask each other if it would not be best to take Him at once and make Him king whether he would or would not consent, but when He saw what they wished to do, He slipped away and went farther up among the hills to rest.

Evening had now come, and the people not finding Jesus, went away to their homes, and the disciples in their little ship returned to Capernaum. The people could not understand, nor could His disciples, that Jesus did not come to be an earthly king over the little nation of the Jews. Not until

FEEDING THE FIVE THOUSAND.

the Holy Spirit came to make all things clear did they understand that He was to be the Spiritual King of all the world.

CHAPTER XXIV.

WALKING THE WAVES—THE TWO KINGDOMS.

While Jesus was alone on the mountain side the disciples were trying to reach Capernaum in their fishing boat. It was not a long sail, but a contrary wind had risen and was blowing them out into the Lake away from the landing place.

They had taken down their sail and were rowing, but by three o'clock in the morning they were still out upon the Lake.

Jesus, who knew all things, saw them struggling with the oars, and coming swiftly down the mountain side He went to them walking upon the water.

The disciples saw a form through the darkness drawing near to them, and strangely enough they did not think of Jesus, but cried out in terror, saying,

"It is a spirit." Then the clear sweet voice of their Master rose over the sound of the wind and the waves, "Be of good cheer, it is I, be not afraid." And Peter, full of glad faith, cried out, "Lord, if it be Thou, bid me come unto Thee on the water."

When Jesus said "Come," Peter climbed over the side of the boat and began to walk toward Jesus, but when a strong wind drove the waves upon him he lost sight of the Lord for a moment, and he was afraid.

"Lord, save me!" he cried, and began to sink.

Then Jesus stretched out His hand and caught Peter, saying, "O thou of little faith, wherefore didst thou doubt?"

When they both entered the ship the wind ceased, and while the disciples wondered and worshipped, saying, "Of a truth Thou art the Son of God," they found themselves at the land not far from Capernaum.

It was on the white beach of pebbles and shells that bordered the plain of Gennesaret where they moored the boat in the early morning, and as soon as the people saw them they began bringing their sick friends to Jesus. Many were too ill to walk, and were brought on little beds or mattresses and laid at Jesus's feet, and there they were healed if they but touched the hem of His garment.

Many of those who brought the sick to Jesus had been with Him on the mountain side, and had eaten of the wonderful bread of heaven that He had broken for them. They believed that He could do anything that He would.

The people whose hearts were set upon making Jesus their king followed Him wherever He went. Some who had been with Him when He made bread for the great company on the hillside at Bethsaida-Julias found Him teaching in the synagogue at Capernaum.

"Teacher, when camest thou hither?" they said. Jesus, knowing that they cared more for His gifts than for His teaching, said, "Ye seek me, not because ye saw the miracles, but because ye did eat of the loaves and were filled," and told them that they should not labor for the food that perishes, but for that which endures forever.

They still wished Him to do some wonder, or show them how to work wonders, for they asked Him what they should do to work the works of God

"This is the work of God," He said, "That ye believe on Him whom He hath sent." Still they remembered the miracle of the bread.

"What sign showest Thou?" they said, "Our fathers did eat manna in the desert." Then He spoke plainly to them of Himself.

"The bread of God is He which cometh down from heaven, and giveth life unto the world." One more spiritual than the rest said reverently, "Lord, evermore give us this bread."

Then Jesus spoke those words about Himself that turned many away from Him. He showed them that He could never be what they expected Him to be—an earthly king. He had only the things of the Spirit to give them, and He called them to a kingdom that could be seen only with spiritual sight.

"I am the bread of life," He said, "He that cometh to me shall never hunger; and he that believeth on me shall never thirst. All that the Father giveth me shall come to me, and him that cometh to me I will in no wise cast out."

The Jews were offended with Him because He had said, "I came down from heaven." "I am the living bread which came down from heaven," He said. "If any man eat of this bread he shall live forever; and the bread that I will give is my flesh which I will give for the life of the world."

Then the Jews were vexed and turned to talk among themselves. They could not understand what He meant, but they saw plainly that He was not going to agree with their plan to make Him the King of the Jews, who would lead them out of their bondage to the Romans, and establish them forever as a nation.

They did not want to follow Him, but they wanted Him to follow their plan. And as for His talk about being the "bread of life,"—"This is an hard saying," they said, "who can hear it?"

While they murmured Jesus said,

"Doth this offend you? What and if you shall see the Son of Man ascending where He was before?"

"*It is the Spirit that quickeneth; the flesh profiteth nothing; the words that I speak unto you, they are Spirit, and they are life.*"

Then they knew that He meant something above what they could see, or what they wanted, and many turned away from Him and went to their homes disappointed. He had said, "there are some of you that believe not," and it was true. Jesus turned to the twelve who stood in silence near Him,

"Will ye also go away?" He said.

Loving, impulsive Peter cried out,

"Lord, to whom shall we go? Thou hast the words of eternal life, and we believe and are sure that Thou art that Christ, the Son of the living God."

"Did I not choose you twelve," said Jesus, "and one of you is a devil."

Already evil spirits had tried to turn Judas away from the Lord by tempting him, and he had let them into his heart. And Jesus, who knew all men, saw them there.

CHAPTER XXV.

A JOURNEY WITH JESUS.

Jesus went away with His disciples into the "borders of Tyre and Sidon." He did not go to the Passover feast, for the anger of the Jews had been growing more violent toward Him and His disciples, and he took the twelve away from the crowded towns around the Lake into the parts that bordered upon a heathen country. He could do far more for the simple-hearted heathen than for Jews who believed themselves to be wise and religious.

When it was known that the young teacher of Nazareth was among them some came to Him who were not Jews. One was a Syrian woman whose

JESUS IN THE WHEAT FIELDS.

daughter was troubled by an evil spirit, and she begged Jesus to have mercy upon her. The disciples were not pleased to have her follow them with strange cries in another language. They believed that the works of Jesus were for the Jews only, and so they begged Him to send her away. Jesus was silent, for He knew all hearts, and saw faith growing in the heart of the poor woman.

He said, trying her faith,

"It is not meet to take the children's bread and cast it to dogs."

"Truth, Lord," she said, "yet the dogs eat of the crumbs which fall from their master's table."

Then Jesus hid Himself no longer from her faith, but said.

"O woman, great is thy faith! be it unto thee even as thou wilt." And her daughter was cured that very hour.

Jesus did not go down by the great sea, though He could see it lying like blue and silver across the west whenever He came to a hilltop as they journeyed, but He went northward to the hills that lie around the mountains of Lebanon. Upon these mountains grew the cedars that Solomon's servants cut down and carried to Jerusalem for the building of the Holy House. They stopped in the Lebanon villages, and came at length to the foot of Mount Hermon, and to the Jordan, crossing over and passing near the place where the great company who followed Jesus had been fed. As they came into Decapolis on the east side of the lake of Gennesaret the people came to Him in crowds again for healing. There He healed a man who could neither hear nor speak.

Coming to Gadara He found crowds coming with their sick for healing. Eight months before He had healed a poor man in whom was a legion of devils, casting them out into a herd of swine, and they had begged Him to leave their coast for they were afraid of Him, but now they were glad to come to Him for healing. No doubt the man who had been healed had told them of the gentleness of Jesus, and of His wonderful words, and had brought many to Him.

It was in Bethsaida-Julias that Jesus once opened the eyes of a blind man. He did not see clearly at first, but when Jesus laid His hand a second time upon his eyes he saw quite well, and was so grateful that he wanted to go and tell all his friends about it, but Jesus told him to go quietly home.

Two blind men followed Him also, crying, "Thou Son of David, have mercy on us!" They followed Him into a house and there Jesus asked, "Believe ye that I am able to do this?" "Yea, Lord," they said.

JESUS WALKING ON THE WAVES.

"According to your faith be it unto you," He said, touching their eyes, and their eyes were opened at once.

Though Jesus had said, "See that no man know it," yet they told it through all that country.

CHAPTER XXVI.

THE CHRISTIAN SABBATH—PETER'S CONFESSION OF FAITH.

Jesus was walking with His disciples one Sabbath day and talking of the Kingdom of Heaven when they came to a field of ripe grain. They had been gathering food for their souls from the teachings of Jesus, and had forgotten to take food for their bodies until they saw the ripe grain and knew that they were hungry. Some of them began to take the heads of wheat (or barley), to rub them in their hands to separate the grain from the chaff, and eat the kernels of wheat.

Following close after them were some men who had been told to watch Jesus and His disciples, and see if anything could be brought against them.

They held very strict views about keeping the Sabbath, as all Pharisees did, and here they saw something that might be called breaking the Sabbath, for were they not really reaping the wheat, and sifting it through their hands?

"Behold thy disciples do that which is not lawful to do upon the Sabbath day," they said. "The Son of Man," said Jesus, "is Lord even of the Sabbath day."

Another Sabbath He entered into a synagogue and taught. Among the people stood a man who had a helpless and withered hand. The same Pharisees who had followed Jesus as spies when He walked through the grain-fields were watching Him in the Synagogue to see if He would heal on the Sabbath. He knew their thoughts, and called the man, saying, "Rise up and stand forth in the midst."

The man rose, and while he stood waiting, Jesus turned to the Pharisees who were eagerly watching to see if Jesus would do something that was forbidden in their law, and said,

"Is it lawful on the Sabbath days to do good, or to do evil? To save life or to destroy it?" The Pharisees dared not answer, and Jesus, looking round upon them all, said to the man, "Stretch forth thy hand."

The man obeyed. Although he had not been able to raise his hand, he stretched it forth, and it became as whole and as strong as the other.

The Pharisees went away very angry, and tried to make a plan among themselves for bringing Jesus into trouble.

Jesus came to fill the law about the Sabbath full of the spirit of heaven; to teach love and service to the neighbor, as well as the love and worship of God, but they could not understand Him.

Jesus was near the end of His ministry to the people east of the Jordan in the country called Decapolis. They were not like the Galilean Jews, they were half heathen people who lived among the wild, rocky hills of that region. They were poor and ignorant, yet they were more ready to accept the gospel than the wise and wicked Pharisees had been.

He had been kind to them in their sickness and poverty, and they followed Him with their sick, and lame, and deaf, and blind, leaving them at His feet until they arose praising God that they had been saved from their sufferings.

Jesus had been teaching in the wild mountain country, and the people would not leave Him to go away to their homes. After three days Jesus said to His disciples, "I have compassion on the multitude because they continue with me now three days and have nothing to eat, and I will not send them away fasting lest they faint by the way."

The disciples did not remember the Lord's power to create bread, and wondered where they should find it in the wilderness to feed such a great multitude.

But when Jesus knew that they had seven loaves of barley bread and a few little fishes He told the people to sit down on the ground, and after giving thanks over the loaves and the fishes, He divided them and gave to His disciples, and the disciples gave to the people. There were four thousand men beside women and children who took the bread that came from the Lord's hands. After all had eaten and were filled they took up seven baskets of the food that was left.

Jesus, though He could create food for the people, taught them to use it wisely and waste nothing.

When the people had been sent to their homes, Jesus, with His disciples, took a fishing boat and crossed the Lake only to find the Pharisees there ready to question Him, and to tempt Him to show them some great sign from heaven.

He told them that they could read the signs of the coming weather in the sky, but they could not see the signs of the times.

Only a wicked people look for a sign, He said, and no sign should be given except the sign that Jonah gave to the Ninevites—a call to repentance.

Then He left them, for He saw the hardness of their hearts.

Again they took their journey in the little ship to the northern end of the Lake, and after landing, followed the east side of Jordan until they passed near the place where the five thousand had been fed by a miracle as they sat on the green hillside.

The disciples found that they had forgotten to bring bread with them. They remembered, perhaps, that they had here eaten the bread that the Lord had created; but the heart of Jesus was heavy with the thought of the unbelief of the people He had come to save, and He said,

"Take heed and beware of the leaven of the Pharisees and the Sadducees."

The disciples did not understand Him, and wondered if He spoke thus because they had not brought bread.

Then Jesus, seeing that they had but little faith, reminded them of the supper on the hillside, when more than five thousand were fed, and of that later meal among the rocky hills of Decapolis, when four thousand and more were fed, and that they did not need to be concerned about food for the body so much as to beware of the false teaching of the Pharisees and of the Sadducees.

They walked still further north, directly toward that beautiful mountain that lifts its head, white with the glistening snow, high above the hills that lead up to it, so that it may be seen over the larger part of Palestine.

They came to Cæsarea Philippi, one of the most beautiful places in the world. It lay in the green lap of Mount Hermon high above the sea, and shut in by cliffs and forests. The upper springs of the Jordan are here. They leap out of a great cavern in the side of the mountain—a river of clear, cold water.

The old Greeks loved the place, and built there a temple to the god of nature, but after the Romans came it was named for the Emperor and Philip the Tetrarch. Here there were more Gentiles than Jews, for it was a gay town in the summer, and people from other towns came to this city of palaces, temples, baths, theatres, and statues. These people did not wish to hear the words of Jesus, but the coolness and beauty of the country around this birthplace of the Jordan made it a fit place to bring His disciples where they could talk over the things of the kingdom without being disturbed by the Pharisees.

Here He was able to pray alone, and once, after prayer, He questioned His disciples about Himself.

"Whom say the people that I am?" He asked. They remembered their talks with the people and said, "John the Baptist, but some say Elias, and others say that one of the old prophets is risen again." "But whom say ye that I am?" He asked. Then Peter, the believing disciple, made his confession of faith,—

"Thou art the Christ, the Son of the living God." Jesus was glad to hear this, for many had come to doubt Him, and many had gone away from Him since they knew that He would not be an earthly king.

"Blessed art thou Simon, son of Jonas," He said, "for flesh and blood hath not revealed it unto thee, but my Father which is in Heaven."

He saw that Peter's faith in the truth was like his name, which means "a rock," and so He said,

"Thou art Peter, and on this rock will I build my church, and the gates of hell shall not prevail against it."

Peter's faith in the truth was also in the hearts of the other disciples for whom He spoke, and Jesus saw that they could now bear what he had to say to them without going away.

He told them that He must soon go to Jerusalem and suffer many things from the chief priests and the scribes and the elders, and that He should be killed by them, and rise again from the dead the third day.

Even Peter's faith was shaken by this. How could the Son of God be killed? He could not believe His Master meant it so.

"Be it far from thee, Lord," he said, "this shall not be unto thee."

Jesus saw the spirit of fear and unbelief rising up in Peter, and to this—not to Peter himself—Jesus said,

"Get thee behind me, Satan; thou art an offence unto me; for thou savourest not the things that be of God, but those that be of men."

Then He plainly told them what they must be ready to meet if they followed Him. They must not hope for any earthly honors or riches, and they must put aside their own wishes and obey the Lord alone.

He told them that whoever wished to live for this world alone would lose all, but whoever was willing to lose all for His sake should find eternal life.

"For what is a man profited," He said, "if he shall gain the whole world and lose his own soul, or what shall a man give in exchange for his soul?"

CHAPTER XXVII.

"AND WE BEHELD HIS GLORY"—A FATHER'S FAITH.

Jesus stayed near Cæsarea Philippi with His disciples for a week. The villagers were cutting the ripe grain, the vineyards were rich with clusters of the rich grapes that grew on the Lebanon hills, and the olives were ripening for the time when they would be put in the presses to make the delicious "oil olive." In that week He must have had many wonderful talks with the villagers.

One evening, as they had come over the lower hills of Hermon, Jesus left the disciples to wait for Him below, taking only Peter and the brothers James and John with Him up the mount. They did not go to the very top but rested on one of the lower peaks. While Jesus went a little distance from them to pray, the three disciples, wrapped in their thick mantles, lay down to wait for Him. In that high clear air they seemed very near heaven. The stars seemed almost as near as the lights in the villages below. They were tired, and watching their Master in prayer, they fell asleep. While they slept they seemed to see a change in the face of Jesus as He prayed. It grew light with a strange inward glory, and all His garments became white and glistening like the snows of Hermon in the sun. They also saw two men with Him whom they seemed to know were Moses and Elias, who had gone to heaven centuries before.

They also heard them talking with Jesus, and they spoke of the same thing that had troubled Peter when Jesus had spoken of it—that He should die at Jerusalem.

They awoke out of sleep, but the vision did not pass away like a dream, they still saw it all.

But as it began to melt away, Peter said, hardly knowing what he said,

"Master, it is good for us to be here, and let us make three tabernacles, one for Thee, and one for Moses, and one for Elias."

Then the glory around Jesus grew until it seemed like a bright cloud at sunset, and it came and wrapt them around in its soft brightness, and they were afraid.

In the silence they heard a Divine voice, saying.

"This is My beloved Son ; hear Him."

When the voice was passed they looked up and saw Jesus there alone. He was bending over them, touching them tenderly, and saying,

"Arise, and be not afraid."

As they came down the mountain He told them to tell no one of the vision until after He had risen from the dead.

It seemed to the disciples, no doubt, like coming down from heaven to earth when after a long walk and talk with Jesus in the summer morning they came near the village they had left, and found the people—among them some Jewish lawyers—disputing with the group of disciples there. As soon as they saw Jesus they all ran to Him, and greeted Him.

One of the men explained what they were disputing about.

"Master," he said, "I have brought unto thee my son which hath a dumb spirit," and he described the frightful state into which it had brought his boy, and added that the disciples could not cast it out.

"Bring him to me," said Jesus, and they brought him, the evil spirit within him throwing him into convulsions as they laid him at Jesus' feet.

"How long is it ago since this came to him?" said Jesus.

"Of a child," said the father, "and ofttimes it hath cast him into the fire and into the waters to destroy him, but if thou canst do anything, have compassion on us, and help us." Jesus said,

"If thou canst believe, all things are possible to him that believeth."

Then the poor father cried out with tears, "Lord, I believe; help thou mine unbelief!"

The Lord did not wait for greater faith than this. He charged the evil spirit to come out of the boy, and after a great struggle it left him as one dead, but Jesus took him by the hand and he arose.

"Why could not we cast him out?" said the disciples afterward.

"This kind," said Jesus, can come forth by nothing but by prayer and fasting."

As they turned their steps toward home—the Lake side in Galilee—Jesus again spoke of the work that lay before Him. The disciples listened sadly, but could not understand why He should speak of being killed, and of rising again from the dead, and they dared not ask Him questions about it.

CHAPTER XXVIII.

THE LORD AND THE LITTLE ONES—LEAVING GALILEE.

As the Lord and His disciples walked over the hills into Galilee some of them fell behind wondering among themselves what He could mean when He spoke of being killed and of rising again. Perhaps they thought it only a sadness that would pass away, and so full of faith in His power were they that they could not believe that One who could raise the dead could Himself die.

"He will be a King," they thought, and began to wonder who among them would be chosen to be greatest in His Kingdom, and even to quarrel about it.

After they had reached Capernaum, and were at home again—probably in Peter's house—Jesus said to them,

"What was it that ye disputed among yourselves by the way?"

There was no word from any one of them, for they were ashamed. Then the Lord sat down, and calling the twelve around Him, said gently,

"If any man desire to be first, the same shall be last of all, and servant of all."

A little child stood near listening, and wishing, perhaps, that he might be a grown man so that he also could be a disciple.

Making room for him in the midst of them all, He called the child, Peter's child, perhaps, who came joyfully to Him. Taking Him tenderly in His arms He said,

"Whosoever shall receive one of such children in my name receiveth me, and whosoever shall receive me, receiveth not me, but Him that sent me."

And He taught His disciples to be humble as a little child in these beautiful words:

"Except ye be converted, and become as little children, ye shall not enter into the Kingdom of Heaven."

"Take heed that ye despise not one of these little ones, for I say unto you that in heaven their angels do always behold the face of my Father which is in heaven."

He also told them of the love of the Father in seeking His lost children. That if a shepherd had but lost one of his hundred sheep, he would leave all the others to go out into the wild mountains to look for the lost sheep. How much more would the Father do for His own, and especially for His little ones.

"Even so," He said, "it is not the will of your Father, which is in heaven, that one of these little ones should perish."

Before going to the Feast at Jerusalem the Lord Jesus said many things to His disciples that would help them to be loving and forgiving toward each other and all the world, for they were very soon going to meet trouble which would try their love and their faith. He told them to deal gently with those who had done wrong, that they might win them back to the right way. He told them that they should have help from heaven when they asked for it, even if there should be only two to ask.

"For where two or three are gathered together in my name," He said, "there am I in the midst of them."

"How oft shall my brother sin against me, and I forgive him?" asked Peter, "till seven times?"

"Until seventy times seven," said Jesus, and He did not mean that we should even count the number of times that we forgive.

Then He told them a story of a forgiving king and an unforgiving servant that you may read in the eighteenth chapter of Matthew.

At the time of the Feast of Tabernacles, the people went up to Jerusalem to offer gifts in the golden Temple for the harvest that the Lord had given them, and to join in a praise service there.

They brought oil, and wine, and wheat, and barley; dates, pomegranates, and figs—something of all they had gathered, and while they marched toward the holy city they sang joyful songs that David had written long before. When they reached Jerusalem they built bowers of branches cut from the trees and lived in them for a week.

Even in the city the people came out of their houses and lived in bowers on the streets and public squares, or upon the flat roofs of the houses, and the hillsides round were covered with the green booths.

The brothers of Jesus came down to Capernaum on their way to the Feast at Jerusalem, and they asked their elder Brother to go also into Judea and show Himself to the world, that His miracles might be seen of all, for they did not believe in Him yet. But Jesus said,

"My time is not yet come, but your time is always ready."

So they went on their journey, and Jesus stayed in Galilee.

After a few days He set His face toward Jerusalem, taking the shortest way through Samaria. The Samaritans were not friendly to the Jews, and the disciples, who had been sent on before to find lodging for the company in a village, were not allowed to bring their Master there.

The gentle John and his brother James were angry that unkindness was shown to Jesus, and wished to call down fire from heaven to destroy the villagers, but Jesus said,

"Ye know not what manner of spirit ye are of, for the Son of Man has not come to destroy men's lives, but to save them."

And they went to another village. On the way they found men who wished to follow Jesus as the disciples did, but while some were ready to leave all, others wished to first bid their friends farewell, or bury their dead, but Jesus saw something in their hearts that showed that they were not fit for the Kingdom of God.

There were many beside the twelve who fully believed in Jesus, and were ready to tell others of the coming kingdom, so He sent them out to all the places where he intended to go, until there were seventy of them preaching the good news. They went, saying, "The Kingdom of God is come unto you," and they healed the sick in Jesus' name. When they returned they were full of joy, saying,

"Lord, even the devils are subject unto us through Thy name." But Jesus said, "Rejoice not that the spirits are subject unto you, but rather rejoice because your names are written in heaven."

CHAPTER XXIX.

AT THE HOUSE OF MARTHA—THE GOOD SHEPHERD.

While Jesus was on His way to Jerusalem a lawyer came and asked Him questions. He did not want to be a disciple, yet he asked what he should do to have eternal life.

Jesus asked him what the commandments said about it, and the lawyer repeated the two great commandments concerning love to the Lord and to the neighbor.

"Thou hast answered right," Jesus replied. "This do and thou shalt live."

"And who is my neighbor?" said the lawyer.

THE MOTHERS OF JERUSALEM.

Then Jesus told a story of a man who went down to Jericho, and was nearly killed by thieves. A priest came that way and when he saw a man who needed help he passed by on the other side of the road. So did a Levite, one of the helpers in the temple worship, but a Samaritan (and the Samaritans were despised by the Jews) came that way, and he stopped in pity for the poor man, dressed his wounds, set him upon his own beast and brought him to an inn and took care of him. When he left the inn he also left money for his care, with the promise of more if it should be needed. Then Jesus asked the lawyer which of these three men was neighbor to him who fell among thieves.

"He that showed mercy on him," said the lawyer. Then said Jesus unto him,

"Go thou and do likewise."

As Jesus came near to Jerusalem He passed through Bethany, a little town at the foot of the Mount of Olives, where perhaps some of His disciples had been preaching the new gospel before Him. There He was gladly received into the house of Martha, who prepared the table with her own hands to offer the best in her house to her honored Guest. She had a brother named Lazarus, who was probably at the feast in Jerusalem, and a younger sister named Mary who loved to listen to every word that Jesus spoke. As every family built a bower of branches during this feast to remind them that for forty years they lived in such houses in the wilderness while coming out of Egypt, there must have been one in the court of Martha's house, and there, perhaps, Jesus rested while Mary sat at His feet and heard His word.

Martha was very busy serving her honored guest, and thought Mary ought to help her in the house, but Jesus said, "Martha, Martha, thou art careful and troubled about many things; but one thing is needful, and Mary hath chosen that good part which shall not be taken away from her."

When the Feast of Tabernacles was at its height Jesus came up to the Temple at Jerusalem. The people had been looking for Him, and as soon as the noble, earnest-faced young Teacher was seen walking in the marble court of the Temple they thronged around Him to hear Him teach, or to see if He would do any miracle.

Some wondered at His wisdom and His doctrine, and asked where it came from. "My doctrine is not mine," He said, "but His that sent me. If any man will do His will he shall know of the doctrine."

He taught them many things that day, and hinted at the same thing that had troubled His disciples, and these were His words,

JESUS IN THE HOUSE AT BETHANY.

"Yet a little while am I with you, and then I go unto Him that sent me. Ye shall seek me and shall not find me, and where I am thither ye cannot come."

The priests, the scribes, and the Pharisees were listening, and He knew that their hearts were too full of pride and self-love to receive His word. They could not go to Him, for they would not let Him come into their hearts.

On the last day, the great day of the Feast, Jesus stood and cried to the people who were about to go back to their homes. His great heart was breaking to bring them into the Kingdom of Heaven, and He knew that they would be scattered as sheep having no shepherd.

"If any man thirst," He cried, "let him come unto me and drink." And He then promised to such as believe the Holy Spirit to dwell in them, and to flow out toward all the world like rivers of living water.

So wonderfully did He preach that many said, "Of a truth this is a prophet," and others said, "This is the Christ," while others were filled with anger and wished to arrest Him. Indeed, when the priests and Pharisees urged the officers to take Him, they said,

"Never man spake like this man," and they would not lay hands on Him.

But Nicodemus, a learned doctor of the law, was a friend of Jesus. He it was who had a talk with Him one night under the olive trees about the Spirit—the breath of God, and he with wise words turned the hatred of the Jews away from Jesus for the time, and they went to their own houses.

Jesus taught in the Temple again the next day, and all the people came to listen.

It was here, perhaps, that the wicked Scribes and Pharisees brought to Him a poor woman who had sinned. They told Him that according to the law she ought to be stoned, and asked what He would say about it. He did not answer, but seemed to be writing on the ground before Him as though He did not hear them. At last, because they would have an answer He looked at them saying,

"He that is without sin among you, let him cast the first stone," and He wrote again on the ground. No one answered Jesus, but one by one they went away too much ashamed to speak. "Hath no man condemned thee?" asked Jesus of the woman standing sorrowful and alone.

"No man, Lord," she said.

"Neither do I condemn thee," He said, "go and sin no more."

Then Jesus sitting in the Treasury of the Temple said,

THE GOOD SAMARITAN.

"I am the light of the world. He that followeth me shall not walk in darkness but shall have the light of life."

Many other things He said that His enemies tried to turn against Him, and the healing on the Sabbath day of a man who had been born blind stirred the anger of the Jews against Him, so that they sought by much questioning to accuse Jesus of sin, not knowing that they were themselves spiritually blind.

But He turned from them to call to the people again as He did on the last day of the Feast, for in His love and pity He longed to bring the lost children of Israel to Himself that He might bless them, as a shepherd brings back the sheep that stray from the fold.

"I am the Good Shepherd; and I know my own, and my own know me," said Jesus, "even as the Father knoweth me, and I know the Father; and I lay down my life for the sheep, and other sheep I have which are not of this fold; them also I must bring, and they shall hear my voice; and they shall become one flock, one Shepherd."

Other beautiful and blessed words He said about the Shepherd and His flock which are written in the tenth chapter of the Gospel of John, but the learned Jews would not listen to Him, and thrice tried to kill Him by stoning Him, but they could not harm Him, for His time had not come.

Then he went away beyond Jordan, where John first baptized, and many believed on Him there.

CHAPTER XXX.

THE LESSON STORIES OF JESUS.

When Jesus was at prayer His disciples stood reverently apart from Him, and one day a disciple came near when he had ceased and said,

"Lord, teach us to pray, as John also taught his disciples."

Then the Lord taught them the beautiful prayer that is now said daily all around the world, and known to every one of us, beginning, "Our Father which art in heaven, Hallowed be Thy name."

And He told them how pleased God is to have His children ask Him for what they need, or come to Him in trouble.

"Ask, and it shall be given you," He said; "seek, and ye shall find; knock and it shall be opened unto you."

THE RETURN OF THE PRODIGAL.

"If a son shall ask bread of any of you that is a father, will he give him a stone? or if he ask a fish, will he for a fish give him a serpent?"

"If ye then, being evil, know how to give good gifts unto your children, how much more shall your Heavenly Father give good gifts to them that ask Him?"

It was while the Lord was teaching in the country called Peræa, east of Jordan, that He told many things that His disciples remembered and wrote in a book afterward, when the Holy Spirit had come to "bring all things to their remembrance," as He had promised.

He had been teaching three years, and was thirty-three years of age.

Some of the people who lived at Bethabara, by Jordan, were present when He was baptized by John, and they were glad to have him stay among them and teach, for they were a kindly people, and though not learned like the men who were often to be found in the Temple courts and in the Synagogues, they were the common people who, hearing the word and loving it, were wiser than the Pharisees.

The Lord told many stories that these people would remember, and afterward understand by the teaching of His Spirit which He said would be given to them. You will read all of them in the Gospels, but here we cannot tell them all.

The story of "The Fig-tree in the Vineyard," "The Great Supper," and "The Foolish Rich Man" were stories of warning to those who were turning away from the things of heaven to the things of the world, and they were meant for all who should read them in the ages of the world.

So were the three stories—they are called "parables" in the Gospels—of the lost things; "The lost sheep," "The lost piece of money," and "The lost son." They were given to us to show the great love of the Heavenly Father for His children, and His constant care in seeking for them when they are wandering away from Him. These stories are the voice of the Father always and everywhere calling His children home, and many a poor soul has turned homeward with tears of repentance after reading them.

One of these stories of lost things will be told here, but it is far more beautiful in the language of the Scriptures.

There was once a rich man who had two sons, and the younger one came to him and said,

"Father, give me the portion of goods that falleth to me."

And so the father divided his property, and gave the younger brother his share. In a few days he had gathered it all together and settled his affairs so that he could go away. He went into a distant country, and there he spent all that he had among bad people who seemed to be his friends, but were really his worst enemies.

When all that he had was spent there came a time of great trouble. There was very little food in the land, for there was a famine, and he was obliged to go to work for the little he could get. It was not easy to find work, for the only thing he could do was to hire himself to a man who kept pigs. His work was to stay in the fields and feed them with husks, the hard pods of the carob tree. Sometimes he was so hungry that he would have been glad to eat even these, but "no man gave unto him." Then the young man "came to himself."

"How many hired servants of my father have bread enough and to spare," he said, "and I perish with hunger!

"I will arise and go to my father, and I will say to him, 'Father, I have sinned against heaven and before thee, and am no more worthy to be called thy son; make me as one of thy hired servants.'"

The father must have been watching for his lost boy, for while he was yet a great way off he saw him, and ran to meet him. He put his arms around him and kissed him without once speaking of his sins, and he called his servants to bring the best robe and put it on him, and a ring for his hand, and shoes for his feet, and then to kill the fatted calf to make a feast for all.

"For," he said "this my son was dead, and is alive again; he was lost, and is found."

The elder son had been away in the field but when he came home heard music and dancing, and called to a servant to ask what these things meant. When he had heard he was very angry, and would not go in. His father came out to beg him to come in and greet his brother, but he said.

"Lo, these many years do I serve thee, neither transgressed I at any time thy commandment, and yet thou never gavest me a kid, that I might make merry with my friends." But the father said,

"Son, thou art ever with me, and all that I have is thine. It was meet that we should make merry and be glad, for this thy brother was dead, and is alive again, and was lost and is found."

There are other stories told by Jesus while in Peræa, which you will find in the gospel by Luke, the beloved physician. One is about the "Unjust Steward," and another is the story of the "Unjust Judge." Still another is called "Dives and Lazarus," or the "Rich man and the Beggar."

The parable of "The Pharisee and the Publican," describes two men who went up into the temple to pray; the one a Pharisee, and the other a publican.

The Pharisee prayed with *himself*, thus, "God, I thank thee that I am not as other men are, or even as this publican. I fast twice a week. I give tithes of all I possess."

And the publican, standing afar off, dared not even lift his eyes to heaven, but smote upon his breast, saying, "God be merciful to me a sinner!"

"This man," said Jesus, "went down to his house justified rather than the other; for every one that exalteth himself shall be abased, and he that humbleth himself shall be exalted."

CHAPTER XXXI.

THE VOICE THAT WAKED THE DEAD—THE CHILDREN OF THE KINGDOM.

While Jesus and His disciples were still east of the Jordan trouble fell upon the happy home in Bethany where Jesus had been an honored guest. A messenger was sent to Jesus in great haste, saying,

"Lord, behold, he whom thou lovest is sick."

It was from Mary and Martha concerning their brother Lazarus.

Jesus sent the messenger back with this message,

"This sickness is not unto death, but for the glory of God, that the Son of God might be glorified thereby," and He remained two days longer where He was. Then He said,

"Let us go into Judea again."

The disciples reminded Him that the Jews there had tried to take His life.

"Our friend Lazarus sleepeth," said Jesus, "but I go that I may awaken him out of sleep."

The disciples thought that if he slept he was doing very well, until Jesus told them plainly,

"Lazarus is dead."

Then Thomas was full of sorrow and said,

"Let us also go that we may die with him."

Bethany was not far from Jerusalem, and when they reached the house of Martha, Lazarus had been dead four days, and was placed in a rock tomb.

JESUS WEPT.

Many Jews from Jerusalem had come out to Bethany to comfort Mary and Martha, and to mourn for their friend Lazarus.

When Martha heard that Jesus was coming she ran to meet Him, but Mary sat still in the house. She thought, perhaps, that He had come too late, and the same thought may have been in Martha's mind when she said,

"Lord, if thou hadst been here my brother had not died, but I know that even now whatsoever thou wilt ask of God, God will give it thee."

"Thy brother shall rise again," said Jesus.

I know that he shall rise again in the resurrection at the last day," she said.

Then Jesus spoke those heavenly words that have been the comfort of the sorrowful ever since,

"I am the resurrection and the life: he that believeth in me, though he were dead, yet shall he live: and whosoever liveth and believeth in me shall never die. Believest thou this?"

"Yea, Lord," answered Martha, "I believe that thou art the Christ, the Son of God which should come into the world."

Then she called Mary quietly, so that the people who were noisily wailing should not hear.

"The Master is come and calleth for thee," she said.

Then Mary rose quickly and went to meet Jesus. The people who were trying to comfort her followed her, for they thought she was going to the tomb to weep there; but they saw her go to meet Jesus and fall at His feet saying, as Martha did,

"Lord, if thou hadst been here, my brother had not died."

When Jesus saw the tears of Mary and her sister and their friends He wept also, not for Lazarus, but His heart was moved for them, and He shared their sorrow.

They brought Him to the tomb—a cave with a stone lying upon it. When He asked them to take away the stone Martha's faith began to fail; but the stone was rolled away, and when Jesus had prayed He called with a loud voice,

"Lazarus, come forth!"

And all who were bending forward toward the low, dark door of the tomb saw a man wrapped in linen come forth from the darkness and try to ascend the stone steps.

"Loose him and let him go," said Jesus. And then there was a scene

THE PHARISEE AND THE PUBLICAN.

so full of sacred joy that John, the disciple, who tells the story, does not show it to us.

After this many believed in Jesus, but others went and told the Pharisees all about it.

It was spring in Peræa, and the valley of the Jordan was full of the singing of birds and the color of blooming trees and wild flowers, while in the fields the young wheat was growing. The people thronged to Jesus in crowds, for He taught them in the open air. The disciples were busy with the people, explaining to the dull, listening to those who wished to ask something of the Master, or keeping back the curious. This had to be done in every village through which they passed. There were many mothers with their children around them who came out of their low white houses to follow Jesus in the way, and to listen when He sat down to teach.

The mothers loved to have the Rabbi's bless their children, for since the days of Abraham, Isaac and Jacob, the blessing of a good man means much to the Israelite.

One day some mothers brought their little ones to Jesus, and begged Him to bless them. The disciples told the mothers to stand back, and not trouble the Master while he was teaching. Jesus knew what they were saying, and He called them unto Him and said,

"Suffer little children to come unto me, and forbid them not, for of such is the Kingdom of God. Verily I say unto you, whosoever shall not receive the Kingdom of God as a little child shall in no wise enter therein."

In this way he made it clear to His disciples, to the mothers, and to all who have read His word since that day, that every child is a citizen of the Lord's Kingdom, and dear to the heart of the King.

Perhaps the mothers had heard that the Lord was about to leave the country east of Jordan to go up to Jerusalem, and they longed to have their little ones share in the blessing they had received while sitting at the feet of the great Teacher and learning of Him, for soon after He crossed the Jordan, and, teaching as he went, set His face toward Jerusalem.

CHAPTER XXXII.

THE YOUNG MAN THAT JESUS LOVED.

A rich young ruler came running after Jesus one day, saying,
"Good Master, what shall I do to inherit eternal life?"
So eager was he to know that he knelt before Jesus by the road side.

Jesus spoke gently to him telling him that God alone is good, and that he knew the commandments that God had given.

"All these have I kept from my youth up," said the young man.

As Jesus looked upon him He saw that he was really trying to be good, and hoping that he could do some great and good act that would give him a certain entrance into heaven. He had been taught by the Rabbis that men were saved by keeping the law and doing outward works of righteousness. He did not know that heaven must begin in his own heart.

Jesus, reading his heart, loved him, and longed to have him know the truth.

"Yet lackest thou one thing," he said, "sell all that thou hast and distribute unto the poor, and thou shalt have treasure in heaven; and come, follow me."

When he heard these words the young man turned away and lost the eager look with which he had come to the Lord's feet. He was very sorrowful, for he was very rich, and he found that he loved his riches more than he loved anything else.

"How hardly," said Jesus, "shall they that have riches enter into the Kingdom of God! For it is easier for a camel to go through a needle's eye than for a rich man to enter the Kingdom of God."

"Who then can be saved?" asked one.

"The things which are impossible with men, are possible with God," He said.

"Lo, we have left all," said Peter, "and followed Thee," and then the Lord gave to His disciples that promise that has been proven true by millions of His children for ages past,—

"There is no man who hath left house or parents, or brethren, or wife, or children for the Kingdom of God's sake, who shall not receive manifold more in this present time, and in the world to come life everlasting."

CHAPTER XXXIII.

THE LAST JOURNEY TO JERUSALEM.

When Jesus and His disciples were finally on the way to Jerusalem Jesus went before them, and the shadow of the great trial He was about to suffer cast its shadow upon Him. The disciples saw it, and Mark says that "they were amazed; and as they followed, they were afraid." He told them all about the trial and the death that lay before Him, but so unwilling were they to believe it, and so sure were they that He would be made king of the Jews, that two of them brought their mother to Jesus to ask that her two sons might sit next to Him when He should come to the throne.

"Ye know not what ye ask," He said, "can ye drink of the cup that I drink of? and be baptized with the baptism that I am baptized with?" and they said,

"We can," not knowing that He spoke of suffering and death.

He told them that though they would indeed drink of His cup, He had no honors to give them.

Then, when the others were vexed with James and John for their foolish request, He talked to them all tenderly about the grace of humility.

"Whosoever of you who will be chiefest," He said, "shall be servant of all. For even the Son of Man came not to be ministered unto, but to minister, and to give His life a ransom for many."

It was the time of the Passover Feast at Jerusalem, and as they crossed at the Fords of Jordan and went over the Jericho plain they must have joined some of the groups of joyful people who were going up to the Feast, some on camels and asses, and some walking beside the beasts bearing tents or merchandise. The valley of the Jordan was bright with the freshness of spring, and as they came near Jericho with its rose-gardens, and orchards, and feathery palms, it looked like the gardens of Paradise. It was sometimes called Jericho "the perfumed" because of its great gardens of roses, and its balsam plantations from which they made perfumes that were sold in all the East. It was warm even in winter there, and no frosts destroyed its tropical fruits and flowers. The rich plain was made fertile by two springs that sent their waters through trenches all through these gardens and orchards. One is called the "Elisha Spring," because the prophet made its poisonous waters pure by casting salt into them.

And so the Passover pilgrims entered Jericho.

There was in Jericho a man named Zaccheus, who, like Matthew of Capernaum, was a rich tax-gatherer. He wanted to see Jesus as He passed, but the crowd was great, and he was a small man, so he ran before the people and climbed up into a sycamore tree to see Him.

As Jesus passed the tree He looked up and said,

"Zaccheus, make haste and come down, for to-day I must abide at thy house."

Zaccheus came down in great haste, and was full of joy to be able to entertain Jesus, though some complained that a sinner should have the honor of taking the Master into his house.

Zaccheus must have heard these cruel remarks, for he said humbly,

"Behold, Lord, the half of my goods I give to the poor; and if I have taken anything from any man by false accusation, I restore him fourfold."

Then Jesus said heartily, "This day is salvation come to this house, forsomuch as he also is a son of Abraham. For the Son of Man is come to seek and to save that which was lost."

It was just outside of Jericho that the bands going out toward Jerusalem passed a blind beggar who cried,

"Jesus, thou Son of David, have mercy on me!"

The Lord heard the cry and called him, and there by the roadside He opened the eyes of Bartimeus to see the beauty all around him, and the kind face of Jesus looking at him. And he followed Him.

The pilgrims came up the steep, rocky road from Jericho to Jerusalem, and they were fortunate who could ride, for the heat was great, and the road hard to climb. Jesus and His friends walked, for they were poor men, as riches are counted in this world.

It was a six hours' journey, and when they reached the green heights of the Mount of Olives they turned aside to the village of Bethany, and there Jesus rested in the house of Mary and Martha and the brother whom He had called back from the grave. The disciples were lodged in the town, no doubt, among their friends, and so grateful and happy were they of Bethany to have the Lord once more among them that they made a supper to show their joy at His coming. It was at the house of Simon, who had been a leper, and cured, perhaps, by Jesus, and Lazarus sat at the table with Jesus, and Mary and Martha served.

It was a holy, happy time, yet shadowed with sadness because of the words of Jesus concerning His death, which the disciples could not believe.

In the midst of the supper Mary brought an alabaster box of very precious and costly perfume, and poured it upon the head of Jesus and also upon His feet, wiping them with her long hair. Judas, one of the twelve, frowned upon her, and said it was a waste, for the perfume might have been sold for money to give to the poor.

But Jesus knew what Mary did.

"Let her alone," He said, "against the day of my burying hath she kept this; for the poor always ye have with you; but me ye have not always."

"She hath done what she could."

"Wheresoever this gospel shall be preached throughout the whole world, this also that she hath done shall be spoken of for a memorial of her."

CHAPTER XXXIV.

THE PRINCE OF PEACE.

It was in the lovely spring time of a land that scarcely knows winter that a strange and beautiful scene made Jerusalem still more beautiful. Over the Mount of Olives, where the olive and the fig-trees were in tender leaf, came a procession of people crying,

"Hosanna; blessed is the King of Israel that cometh in the name of the Lord!"

The road was crowded with people who with lifted faces and songs of praise waved branches of palm as they walked before and beside Jesus, who was riding toward Jerusalem, seated upon a young ass, after the manner of the kings and prophets of ancient Israel.

After Jesus and His friends had left Bethany to go to Jerusalem He had sent two of His disciples to a village near by to bring to Him an ass, with its colt, that they would find tied there, and they were to say to the owner of the asses, "The Lord hath need of them," that the words of the prophet might be fulfilled,

"Tell ye the daughter of Zion, 'Behold thy king cometh unto thee, meek, and sitting upon an ass, and a colt, the foal of an ass.'"

While the Lord and His friends were coming up the Mount of Olives, many people from Jerusalem who knew that He was on His way came to meet Him, and when the two disciples brought to Jesus the ass upon which He was to ride they placed Him upon it, and spreading their garments in the way, and with waving palms and singing they came over the ridge of the Mount of Olives from which they could see Mount Zion shining before them. The Pharisees had come out to see what it meant and were angry. "See—the world is gone after Him!" they said, but Jesus, when they asked Him to stop the praises of the people, told them that the very stones would cry out if the people should hold their peace. As they came to a point in the road where from a smooth rocky height they could see the great city with its temple before them, the whole company stopped, and Jesus, beholding it, wept over it saying,

"If thou hadst known, even thou, in this thy day, the things which belong to thy peace, but now they are hid from thine eyes!"

And He spoke of the days when enemies should surround the Holy City, and lay it even with the ground, because they knew not the time of their visitation. Fifty years after the Romans took the Holy City and burned the beautiful Temple, and put uncounted people to death. And so Jesus went down through the valley of the Kedron and up through the city gates with the great procession that grew at every step until He came to His Father's House—the Temple. Then He looked about and saw the buyers and sellers again making the Temple a market, but He went silently away with His friends to Bethany again. He had entered the city as the Prince of Peace, not as a Roman Emperor would do, with sound of trumpet and the tread of armed legions, and they knew not the time of their visitation.

CHAPTER XXXV.

THE CHILDREN IN THE TEMPLE.

The next morning Jesus went early with His disciples to the Temple. It was on the way as they went over the Mount of Olives that they passed a barren fig-tree—one that bore nothing but leaves. It was like the Pharisees, who outwardly seemed to be religious, but were inwardly evil, and bore none of the fruits of a religious life.

"Let no fruit grow on thee henceforward forever," said Jesus, and it withered away. When the disciples wondered, Jesus said,

"If ye have faith, and doubt not, ye shall not only do this which is done to the fig-tree, but also if ye shall say unto this mountain, 'Be thou removed, and be thou cast into the sea,' it shall be done. And all things whatsoever ye shall ask in prayer, believing, ye shall receive." When Jesus came again to the Temple He drove out the buyers and sellers and the money-changers, as He had done before.

"It is written," He said, "'My house is the house of prayer, but ye have made it a den of thieves.'"

When they had been driven out, the people who had been waiting for Jesus, and the blind and the lame came to Him, and He healed all who came. The Pharisees looked on with hatred in their hearts, and talked with the priests of arresting Him then and there, but a clear, sweet sound of young voices singing came floating through the temple courts, and they saw bands of children who were crying, "Hosanna to the Son of David!" and it rang like heavenly music through all the place.

"Hearest thou what these say?" cried the angry Pharisees, and Jesus answered, "Yea; have ye never read, 'Out of the mouths of babes and sucklings thou hast perfected praise?'" Then He left them and went again to Bethany to rest in the house of His faithful friends, Martha, and Mary, and Lazarus.

CHAPTER XXXVI.

THE LAST DAY IN THE TEMPLE.

It was on a Tuesday that Jesus came again early to the Temple. It was the last day of His teaching there and He filled it with wonderful sayings that have been taught in thousands of Christian temples for nearly two thousand years. The chief priests and elders, who were full of anger because He had acted as if He had a right to say who should come into the Temple courts, came to Him as He was teaching and said,

"By what authority doest thou these things? and who gave thee this authority?" Jesus answered them by asking a question, "The baptism of John, whence was it? from heaven, or of men?" They could not answer, for

"HOSANNA!"

they said in their own minds, "If we shall say 'From heaven,' He will say, 'Why did you not then believe him;' but if we shall say 'Of men,' we fear the people, for all men hold John as a prophet." And so they said, "We cannot tell."

And Jesus answered, "Neither tell I you by what authority I do these things." They could not find what they wanted—something to accuse Him of before the Jewish Council and so they tried to lead Him to say something that would turn the Romans against Him. They came to Him with flattering words, saying that they knew that He taught the way of God truly, and would He tell them if it was lawful to give tribute to Cæsar or not? He saw their deceit and cunning, and said, "Why tempt ye me? Show me a penny. Whose image and superscription is this?" They told Him it was Cæsars. "Render therefore," He said, "unto Cæsar the things which be Cæsars, and to God the things which be God's."

They wondered much at the wisdom of His answer, and could find nothing whereof to accuse Him, but perhaps they never knew what He really meant to say to them—and to us also—that His Kingdom was not of this world.

CHAPTER XXXVII.

THE LAST WORDS IN THE TEMPLE.

On this day also, as Jesus sat near the treasury of the Temple and saw the rich, and the self-righteous casting their money into the boxes placed there, He saw a poor widow come with her mourning dress showing that she was the poorest of the poor—a pauper—and yet she had something to give: she dropped two "mites" into one of the boxes under the marble colonnade that surrounded the court of the women. Taken together these two coins were worth much less than a penny, but they were "all her living," and though the Lord did not speak to her, as far as we know, He saw her faith, and His blessing must have reached her in ways that we know nothing about. To those who stood about Him He said, "Of a truth I say unto you that this poor widow hath cast in more than they all; for all these have of their abundance cast into the offerings of God; but she of her penury hath cast in all the living that she had."

Jesus, who "spake as never man spake," preached the new Gospel of the Kingdom by means of stories, or parables, and on one long day of teach-

SHOWING THE PENNY.

ing in the Temple He told several stories that the people never forgot. Two of them were stories of the vineyard. One of them was of a man who sent his two sons into his vineyard to work. One answered "I will not," but afterward repented and went, while the other, who had said "I go sir," went not. Jesus taught in this that real sinners who at first refuse to enter God's kingdom but afterward repent and enter, are better than the heartless hypocrites who talk much of their religion but are inwardly evil.

The other story was of a certain householder who owned a vineyard and let it out to some men while he took a journey into a far country. When the time of the fruit drew near he sent his servants to the men who had rented the vineyard, that they might receive the fruits of it, but the men beat one servant, and stoned another, and killed another. When the owner sent other servants they treated them in the same way. Then he sent his son saying, "They will reverence my son," but the men determined to kill the heir and take the vineyard for themselves, and they cast out the son of the lord of the vineyard and killed him. In this story He spoke of His own death, as well as that of the prophets and John the Baptist before Him.

The chief priests and Pharisees, when they heard this parable knew that the Lord spoke of them, and they tried again to take Him by force, but feared the people.

Another story told in the Temple that day was of the "Marriage of the King's Son" which you will find in the twenty-second chapter of Matthew. It shows first how the Jews were asked into the Kingdom of Christ, but refused to come, and their city was given over to their enemies to destroy. In the second part of the parable the call of all nations to come into Christ's kingdom is described, and the man who was found at the feast without a wedding garment, describes those who come into the church without real faith in the Lord Jesus, and are not prepared to enter heaven. "For many are called," said Jesus, "but few are chosen."

Knowing the wickedness of the priests and Pharisees, who stood before the people as more holy than others, the Lord ended His last day in the Temple with words to them that must have been sharper than a sword, and more burning than flames of fire. These words are in the twenty-third chapter of Matthew, and may no child who reads them ever live to deserve to hear them for himself. To the hypocrite alone the Lord was stern and severe, but to the sinner who truly repented He was full of forgiving love. After telling them of the sorrows and desolations that must fall upon the Holy City because of the sins of those who should be true and faithful teachers of their holy

THE TWO MITES.

religion, He sent forth these last words of love and sorrow through the Temple courts.

"O Jerusalem, Jerusalem, thou that killest the prophets and stonest them which are sent unto thee, how often would I have gathered thy children together, even as a hen gathereth her chickens under her wings, and ye would not! Behold your house is left unto you desolate, for I say unto you, ye shall not see me henceforth till ye shall say, 'Blessed is He that cometh in the name of the Lord.'" And He went out of the Temple to return no more.

CHAPTER XXXVIII.

AN EVENING ON THE MOUNT OF OLIVES.

Jesus and His friends went out from the Temple and Jerusalem to the Mount of Olives, and as they looked back upon the beautiful buildings of marble and gold that made the Temple seem like a great jewel shining in the sunset, the disciples turned to Jesus and spoke of it, but He said,

"There shall not be left here one stone that shall not be thrown down."

They sat down on the slope of Olivet where the olive and fig-trees were putting forth their new leaves, and in that quiet time Peter, and James, and John, and Andrew drew close about their beloved Master, and said, "Tell us, when shall these things be, and what shall be the sign of thy coming, and the end of the world?" He told them many things hard to be understood; of the sorrows of Israel when their city should be destroyed, and the people scattered; of the end of the age, when they should turn to the Lord they had rejected, and of His coming to the whole world.

"Watch, therefore," He said, "for ye know not what hour your Lord doth come," and He told them of the faithful and the unfaithful servants; that the one was found doing his duty when his lord returned, and was made ruler over all his goods, but the other, unfaithful in all things, was surprised by his lord's coming and cast out.

He told them another beautiful "watching" story of the Ten Virgins who went forth with their little lamps to meet the bridegroom on his way to the marriage feast. Five of them took oil to fill their lamps, and five took no oil with them. The bridegroom was long in coming, and they all fell asleep; but at midnight there was a cry, "Behold the bridegroom cometh! go ye out to meet him!" Then they all arose and trimmed their lamps, but five of the lamps had gone out, and the foolish maids who brought no oil to fill them begged it of the others, but they were told that they must go and buy it of those who had it to sell. While they went to buy the bridegroom came, and they that were ready went in with him to the marriage, and the door was shut. Afterward, when the five thoughtless ones came to the door crying, "Lord, Lord, open to us!" they only heard the answer, "I know you not."

After this He told them the story of the Talents, which you may read in the twenty-fifth chapter of Matthew. It is the Lord's teaching to all disciples about making the most of the life He gives us.

His last story was a picture of the gathering of the nations, and the separation of the good and the true from the false and the evil. The King's call to the good, "Come ye blessed of my Father, inherit the kingdom prepared for you from the foundation of the world," carried with it a strange reason. "For I was an hungered, and ye gave me meat; I was thirsty, and ye gave me drink; I was a stranger, and ye took me in; naked, and ye clothed me; I was sick, and ye visited me; I was in prison, and ye came unto me."

Then the good whom He had called were astonished, and cried, "Lord, when saw we thee an hungered and fed thee? or thirsty, a stranger, sick, or in prison?" and He answered, "Inasmuch as ye have done it unto one of the least of these my brethren, ye have done it unto me." To the false and the evil He could not say these things, but quite the opposite; and when they wondered when they had seen the Lord hungry, or thirsty, or a stranger, or naked, or sick, or in prison, and had not ministered unto Him, He said, "Inasmuch as ye did it not to one of the least of these, ye did it not to me." Those by a life of love and service had chosen eternal life, but these by a life of selfishness had chosen death.

CHAPTER XXXIX.

THE HOLY SUPPER.

There were two more days before the Passover Feast when Jesus would eat the Paschal Supper with His disciples. He spent the time with them trying to help them to bear the great trial that was before them, and which would shake their faith in Him to the utmost. They still believed that some great miracle would break around them like light in the darkness, and that Jesus would be acknowledged as the Messiah for whom the whole nation was waiting and yet the shadow grew deeper. The faith of one had failed. Judas had secretly hoped that Jesus would be made king, and that His disciples would be honored with riches and power, but little by little this hope had been dying, and little by little his heart had been turning away from his Master and his brethren, until, with the resolve to forsake the Lord, he opened the door of his heart to Satan, who began to enter in and possess him.

The high priest and the elders were plotting against Jesus in their council, and Judas, leaving Bethany and the company of the Lord and His disciples, went over the road he had so often walked with Jesus with a thought from Satan burning in his heart. He loved money more than everything else, and there was but one thing that would bring it now since all hope of Jesus becoming a king was past.

He went to the Temple and asked to be taken before the rulers, and he said to them, "What will ye give me, and I will deliver Him unto you?" There was a bargain made at once, and out of the Temple treasury they weighed him thirty pieces of silver, and he carried them away with the promise that he would watch Jesus, and tell them when and where they could take Him. He did not remember that five hundred years before the prophet Zechariah had written, "So they weighed for my price thirty pieces of silver."

On Thursday morning, the first day of the Feast, Jesus sent Peter and John to prepare a place where He should hold the Paschal Supper with His disciples in the evening. He told them to go into the city, and there they would meet a man bearing a pitcher of water, and if they would follow him he would show them a large upper room furnished. There they were to make ready the Passover.

They found it as He had said, and when the lamb had been slain at the Temple, the feast prepared, and the hour was come, the Lord sat down with the twelve. It was the last time that He would break the bread of the Passover with them before He suffered, and it was to be the first Holy Supper of the Christian Church. "With desire I have desired to eat this Passover with you before I suffer;" He said, "for I say unto you that I will not any more eat thereof until it be fulfilled in the Kingdom of God." Before Him were the cakes of unleavened bread, the wine, the water and the herbs, while the Paschal Lamb was on a side table. After the blessing and the thanks, the Lord filled a cup with wine and water, and blessing and tasting it passed it to His disciples. It was the custom for the master of the feast to wash his hands at this point, and Jesus rose, and laid aside His tunic, and tying a long towel around His waist, poured water into a large basin and going to His disciples knelt down to wash their feet. They had been contending as to who should sit nearest to the Lord, and so be accounted greatest, and He thus taught them a lesson of humility. He told them that they were not to be among those who hold authority. "But he that is greatest among you let him be as the younger," He said, "and he that is chief as he that doth serve." The disciples looked on astonished and distressed, for their Master was doing the work that slaves were in the habit of doing, and Peter cried, "Lord, dost *thou* wash *my* feet?" Jesus said gently, "What I do thou knowest not now, but thou shalt know hereafter." "Thou shalt never wash my feet;" said the loving, impulsive Peter, and Jesus answered, "If I wash thee not thou hast no part with me." "Lord, not my feet only," the humbled disciple said, "but also my hands and my head!" When He sat down with them again He talked tenderly to them of serving each other as He had served them, adding, "If ye know these things, happy are ye if ye do them." With a troubled spirit He said, "Behold, the hand of him that betrayeth me is with me on the table." Then the disciples began to inquire sorrowfully among themselves who it could be, and to ask the Lord in turn, "Is it I?" Even Judas, close beside Him, asked the same question, but the disciples did not hear the Lord's reply. Peter, beckoning to John, signed to him to ask the Master, for John sat next the Lord, and leaned upon His breast. When he asked, "Lord, who is it?" Jesus said, perhaps in a whisper to John.

"He it is to whom I shall give a sop when I have dipped it," and He gave it to Judas Iscariot. Then Satan entered fully into the angry, covetous heart of Judas, and when Jesus said to him in a low voice, "That thou doest do quickly," he rose and went out into the night. Alone with His faithful friends, the Lord took bread and blessed it and broke it, and gave to them, saying, "Take, eat, this is my body; this do in remembrance of me." And He took the cup, saying, "Drink ye all of it, for this is my blood of the New Testament, which is shed for many for the remission of sins."

And so the Lord founded the Holy Supper of His Church, the mystery and the holiness of which you will know more and more as you grow in the heavenly life, and receive through His Spirit the new wine of the Kingdom. John, the beloved disciple, kept for us the wonderful and precious words that the Lord spoke after the Holy Supper. They are full of a love for His children so deep and wide that we can never hope to measure it. They are written in the fourteenth, fifteenth, sixteenth, and seventeenth chapters of John's Gospel, and every child should hide them in his memory and heart before he is grown, and in after life they will be bread in time of spiritual famine.

Looking around upon their troubled faces at the table the Lord said to His disciples. "Let not your heart be troubled; ye believe in God, believe also in me. In my Father's house are many mansions. I go to prepare a place for you. And if I go and prepare a place for you, I will come again and receive you unto myself, that when I am there ye may be also." He answered their questions, and He promised them the Comforter—the Holy Spirit of Truth, who would teach them all things, and make all the dark things clear. He also promised certainly to come back to them and not leave them orphans.

After they had sung a psalm they arose from the table, but they lingered for the Lord's last words and His prayer. He charged them to be steadfast and live from Him, as a branch lives from the vine, for He was the true spiritual Vine, and without Him they could do nothing. He told them of His great love for them, and that they must love one another through all the suffering and persecution that was before them, and trust to the Spirit of Truth, who would guide them in all things, and teach them the things He would say to them, but which they were not yet able to bear. And He promised that whatever they should ask the Father in His name should be given them. Then lifting up His eyes to heaven He prayed for His disciples, and for all disciples who should believe on Him through their word, that they might be one with each other and with Him as He was one with the Father, and, being made clean from the evil that is in the world that they should be with Him forever in heaven. After the prayer they went out of the city, and over the brook Kedron into a garden where Jesus had often sat with His disciples.

CHAPTER XL.

THE NIGHT OF THE BETRAYAL.

As they went out through the darkness down the valley and over the Kedron, Jesus still talked with His disciples. To Peter's question, "Lord, where goest thou?" He said, "Whither I go thou canst not follow me now, but thou shalt follow me afterwards." "Lord, why cannot I follow thee now?" said Peter. "I will lay down my life for thy sake."

"Verily, verily I say unto thee, the cock shall not crow till thou hast denied me thrice," said Jesus.

"Simon, Simon, behold Satan hath desired to have you that he may sift

THE HOLY SUPPER.

you as wheat; but I have prayed for thee that thy faith fail not; and when thou art converted, strengthen thy brethren."

"All ye shall be offended because of me this night; for it is written, 'I will smite the Shepherd, and the sheep of the flock shall be scattered abroad.'"

Jesus and his friends had reached the olive trees of Gethsemane when He asked them to sit there while He went away a little distance to pray. He took Peter and James and John with Him; and began to be very sorrowful, and He said,

"My soul is exceeding sorrowful, even unto death: tarry ye here and watch with me." He went a little farther, and fell on His face and prayed, saying, "O my Father, if it be possible, let this cup pass from me: nevertheless, not as I will, but as Thou wilt." He found His disciples sleeping for sorrow, and He said to Peter, "What! could ye not watch with me one hour? Watch and pray, lest ye enter into temptation." Again He prayed, "O my Father, if this cup may not pass away from me except I drink it, Thy will be done." And there appeared an angel unto Him from heaven, strengthening Him. Then there was the sound of the tread of many feet, and the light of torches moving among the olive trees, and Judas, leading a band of priests, elders and captains of the Temple came toward the little group, and kissed Jesus as a sign that He was the One whom they sought. Jesus turned to him saying, "Judas, betrayest thou the Son of Man with a kiss?" And to the others, "Whom seek ye?"

"Jesus of Nazareth," they answered. And when Jesus had said to them, "I am He," they fell backward at the sight of His face. "When I was daily with you in the Temple," He said, "ye stretched forth no hands against me; but this is your hour and the power of darkness." Peter drew a sword and struck at the high priest's servant in defence of his Master, but Jesus said gently,

"Suffer ye thus far," and touched his ear and healed him. "Put up thy sword into the sheath," He added. "The cup which my Father hath given me, shall I not drink it?"

Then they took Jesus and bound Him to lead Him away, and the disciples forsook Him and fled, as had been written in the prophets. But John, the loving and beloved, came back and followed Jesus. So did Peter, remembering his vow, but he followed Him afar off.

GETHSEMANE.

CHAPTER XLI.

DESPISED AND REJECTED OF MEN.

Jesus was first taken to Annas, the old High-Priest, who sent Him bound to Caiaphas, who was his son-in-law, and High-Priest that year.

John went in with Jesus to the palace of the High-Priest, but Peter stood outside the door, shivering with the chill of the night, but more with fear.

A servant girl at the door said, when John came out to bring him in,

"Art not thou also one of this man's disciples?"

And Peter said, "I am not."

Restless and unhappy, he walked about, or warmed himself by the fire, until three had accused him of being a follower of Jesus, and three times he had denied his Lord. Then there came a sound that struck him through—he heard through the open windows the crowing of a cock. It had crowed once before, but he did not think then of what the Lord had said, but now his memory and conscience were wide awake, for, as he looked over the heads of the people towards Jesus standing bound and alone before the High-Priest, the Lord turned and looked upon Peter. That look broke Peter's heart, and he rushed out of the place, and wept bitterly.

There was a mock trial which would pain the heart of a child to dwell upon, and which we will not describe at length. It is enough to know that the Lamb of God, who had come to take away the sins of the world, was willingly in the power of His enemies, and going down to death. A wonderful description of the trial and death of the Messiah may be found in the fifty-third chapter of Isaiah, which was fulfilled in the trial and death of Jesus. The hatred of the priests, the scoffings, the blows, and the cruel words of the people we will not describe. "He was oppressed, and He was afflicted, yet He opened not His mouth. He is brought as a lamb to the slaughter, and as a sheep before her shearers is dumb, so He opened not His mouth." Finally Caiaphas cried,

"I adjure thee by the living God, that thou tell us whether thou be the Christ, the Son of God!" Jesus said,

"I am; and ye shall see the Son of Man sitting on the right hand of power, and coming in the clouds of heaven."

Then the High Priest rent his garments as if shocked at such profanity, and said,

JESUS BETRAYED BY JUDAS.

"Ye have heard the blasphemy; what think ye?" And they all condemned Him to be guilty of death.

There was another gathering of the priests in the morning as the day began to dawn. There were more cruel words and blows for the Divine Man who was bearing the sins of the world, and He was taken away to Pilate.

And where was the wretched man who had sold his Master into the hands of His enemies?

He could not have thought that he was bringing death on His Master; but when at last he saw the Lord coming, pale, suffering and bound, down the marble steps, and heard "Death! death!" on every side, he became terrified. He had no one to turn to, for he had not a friend among men. He ran to the Temple and, finding some priests, begged them take back the money they had given him, saying, "I have sinned, in that I have betrayed the innocent blood."

"What is that to us," said the heartless priests. "See thou to that."

Then Judas cast the thirty pieces of silver over the marble floor, and fled from the place. Afterward he was found outside the city, where he had hanged himself. The priests could not put the price of blood in the Lord's treasury, and so they bought with it a field in which to bury strangers.

CHAPTER XLII.

THE KING OF HEAVEN AT THE BAR OF PILATE.

Pilate, the Roman Governor, who had come up from Cæsarea by the sea to keep order in Jerusalem during the Passover, was in his fine palace called "The Prætorium." Adjoining was "The Hall of Judgment," where cases were brought to the Governor to be judged, and just outside this Hall was a place called "The Pavement." It was a broad floor of many-colored marbles, open toward the city, and having an ivory judgment-seat.

While the morning was lighting the gold of the Temple roof to splendor, there was a deep shadow over the friends of Jesus. Their Lord was being led through the streets of Jerusalem by Roman guards, condemned to die. His mother and the women who believed in Him were in the city and saw Him, perhaps, as He was hurried by, pale and weak from the cruelty of wicked men. The priests would not go into the Judgment Hall for fear of defilement at the time of their Feast, so Pilate came out to "The Pavement"

JESUS CROWNED WITH THORNS.

and sat down upon the ivory judgment seat. He was a stern, proud man wearing a white toga with a rich purple border—the robe of a Roman ruler.

"What accusation do you bring against this man," asked Pilate, looking at the pure, pallid face of the Divine Man, and turning to the dark and evil faces of His accusers. To their complaining remark, "If he were not a malefactor we would not have delivered him up unto thee," Pilate replied,

"Take ye him and judge him according to your law."

When they replied that (under Roman rule) it was not lawful for them to put any man to death, Pilate did not wish to condemn that just One of whom he had known nothing but good, for he had heard of His miracles, and had doubtless heard his wife speak of the young Rabbi. He rose and went into the Hall, ordering the guards to bring Jesus to him. Then he questioned Him,

"Art thou the King of the Jews?" he asked.

"My Kingdom is not of this world," said Jesus. "If my Kingdom was of this world, then would my servants fight, that I should not be delivered to the Jews; but now my Kingdom is not from hence."

"Art thou a king then?" said Pilate.

"Thou sayest that I am a king. To this end was I born, and for this cause came I into the world, that I should bear witness unto the truth. Every one that is of the truth heareth my voice."

"What is truth?" said Pilate, wondering, perhaps, what kingdom of truth this harmless man was dreaming of, and then he rose and went forth to the people on "The Pavement" who were saying that this man was stirring up the people from Galilee to Jerusalem.

Pilate, hearing that Jesus was a Galilean, sent him to the palace of Herod Antipas, who ruled over that province, and who was now in Jerusalem, but He was sent back to Pilate crowned with thorns and wearing a faded purple robe. The Roman soldiers had jested about His kingship, and Antipas had cruelly carried it out in returning Him in this dress to Pilate, through the streets of the city. He had been tried the fourth time and now Pilate made another effort to set Him free. He questioned Him again and heard the complaints of the Jews, but Jesus would not defend Himself.

"Hearest thou not how many things they witness against thee?" said Pilate. "Answerest thou nothing?" If Jesus would only defend Himself!

Then Pilate thought he would scourge Jesus to satisfy His enemies, and let Him go.

"Ye have brought this man unto me," he said to the chief priests, "as one that perverteth the people, and behold, I, having examined him before you,

THE SIN OF PETER.

have found no fault in this man. No, nor yet Herod. I will therefore chastise him and release him."

The cry of "Crucify him! crucify him!" rose again.

A message was sent to Pilate from his wife, which deepened the shadow on his face. "Have thou nothing to do with that just man," she said, "for I have suffered many things this day in a dream because of him."

The people had been persuaded by the priests to ask for Barabbas, and when Pilate asked which of the two he should release to them, they cried,

"Barabbas!"

"What shall I do with Jesus, which is called Christ?" and all cried,

"Let him be crucified!"

"Why, what evil hath he done?" asked Pilate, but the cry was so great he could bear it no longer, and calling a slave to bring water, he washed his hands before them as a sign that he took no blame for the act, and said,

"I am innocent of the blood of this just person: see ye to it." but they cried,

"His blood be upon us, and upon our children." And when Pilate had given the order to scourge and crucify Jesus, he went into his palace.

CHAPTER XLIII.

LOVE AND DEATH.

Jesus had been meeting and conquering evil all His life, and in the last hour of it the last enemy was overcome. There were no children at the cross when Jesus laid down His life for us all, and we will not lead you there to point out all the means used by evil men to increase the suffering of our Lord. It was greatest within the great Heart of Love which broke for the sins of the world, and when you have learned the nature of Spirit you will be able to understand that Jesus chose to pass through an earthly life of poverty and temptation, and die a painful and shameful death, that He might be the Brother of the poor, the tempted, the suffering and the dying. "He was taken from prison and from judgment;" "He poured out His soul unto death, and was numbered with the transgressors;" "He bore the sins of many, and made intercession for the transgressors." So Isaiah wrote of the coming Messiah seven hundred years before. But so blind were the

"ART THOU A KING?"

Jews that they could not see that the Redeemer had come to Zion. "He came unto His own and His own received Him not."

Bearing His cross He went forth meekly to death, and when He fell beneath the heavy cross, the Roman soldiers forced a passing stranger to carry it. All along the street women wept for pity as He passed, and there was sorrow in many hearts for the Man whom they had believed in as the One who was to deliver their nation.

But the eleven disciples—where were they? In deep grief somewhere; but only one—John the Beloved—followed his Master down to death. With the suffering mother of Jesus and the faithful women disciples he kept near his Lord. They saw the rough soldiers as they took the Lord's garments and divided them among themselves, and when they put His body upon the cross they heard Him pray,

"Father, forgive them, for they know not what they do!"

Two robbers were crucified with Jesus, upon His right hand and on His left. One begged Him to save him, and reviled Him because He did not; but the other said, "Lord, remember me when Thou comest into Thy Kingdom." And Jesus said, "Verily I say unto thee, To-day shalt thou be with me in Paradise."

His dying eyes also beheld His mother standing by the cross with the beloved John and the faithful women who had been His friends. The hour had come spoken of by Simeon in the Temple when he said, "Yea a sword shall pierce through thy own soul also." Jesus, looking at His mother supported by John said,

"Woman, behold thy son!" And to the disciple He said, "Son, behold thy mother!" And from that hour John took her to his own home to love and care for her through the rest of her life.

We will not look at the darkness that rolled over the sky, shutting out the light of the sun, or the sights and sounds of that day on Calvary. Jesus, thinking of the redemption He had wrought out for us, bowed His head and said,

"It is finished! Father, into Thy hands I commend my spirit." Then the great veil before the Holy Place in the Temple was torn in two from the top to the bottom, as a sign that the Lord Jesus by His death had opened the way for us into life eternal.

JESUS BEARING THE CROSS.

CHAPTER XLIV

LOVE AND LIFE.

There was a good man of Arimathea named Joseph who was a disciple of Jesus, but not a fearless one. He had not followed Jesus with the twelve, but he had loved Him, and when he knew that his Master, who had not where to lay His head in life, had not a place of burial in death, he lost all fear and went to Pilate and begged the body of Jesus. This Pilate willingly gave him, and he, bringing helpers, took the body from the cross and tenderly brought it to his own garden in which was a new tomb hewn out of the rock. In this peaceful garden-room for the dead they laid Him, wrapped Him in fine linen and spices, for another disciple who had not dared to follow Jesus openly had come with a mixture of myrrh and aloes of a hundred pounds weight to embalm the body of Jesus. This was Nicodemus who had a talk with Jesus by night among the olive trees about the breath of God in man. So these two rich men buried Jesus, and a prophecy was fulfilled.

We do not know that any of the eleven disciples helped to bury Jesus, but, while John took the mother of Jesus to a place of rest and safety, his own mother, Salome, and Mary, the mother of James, and Mary Magdalene stood looking on afar off. There were other women also, who helped to guard the body of the crucified Lord when it seemed to be forsaken of all men. They marked the place where He lay and went away, for the hours of "preparation" and the Sabbath were before them. On the eve of Friday they "prepared spices and ointments, and rested the Sabbath day (seventh day) according to the commandment. But Roman soldiers came and set a seal upon the tomb, and watched it night and day. On the first day of the week (now the Christian Sabbath) very early in the morning, while the streets were still, and there lay only a faint streak of rose in the purple east, Mary Magdalene hastened out of the city to the tomb in the garden, bearing her spices. When she reached the place she saw no guards there, and the heavy stone was rolled away from the door of the tomb. A great fear fell upon the woman who "loved much," and she ran to find Peter and John. "They have taken away the Lord out of the sepulchre," she said, "and we know not where they have laid Him."

Then Peter and John ran, and John the loving ran faster than Peter the believing, and was the first to reach the tomb. The other women also had

THE DESCENT FROM THE CROSS.

gone to the tomb early bearing their spices for the embalming, wondering on the way who should roll away for them the great stone that stood at the door of the tomb. But they found the stone rolled past the door, and entering the low vestibule they saw a vision of an angel, in a long white garment, and were afraid.

"Ye seek Jesus of Nazareth which was crucified," he said; "He is risen; He is not here: behold the place where they laid Him. But go your way, tell His disciples and Peter that He goeth before you into Galilee; there shall ye see Him, as He said unto you."

The Lord had left a special message for Peter who had denied Him so cruelly and had repented so thoroughly! As they looked to "behold the place where they laid Him," they saw another angel shining white through the gloom, "one at the head, and the other at the feet where the body of Jesus had lain." They also ran, glad, yet half afraid, to tell the disciples what they had seen and heard.

Peter and John found the linen that had wrapped the Lord's body laid carefully aside. They did not yet remember the prophecy concerning His resurrection from the dead, but they believed He had risen, and they went away, hoping perhaps, that He was seeking them.

Mary Magdalene could not leave the empty tomb until she had learned something more about the Lord. Weeping and desolate she stood at the low door of the cave-tomb, and stooping to look in again she saw the vision of angels that the other women had seen, "one at the head and the other at the feet, where the body of Jesus had lain."

"Why weepest thou?" they asked, and she answered,

"Because they have taken away my Lord, and I know not where they have laid Him." As she turned to go out into the garden she saw one standing there who said,

"Woman why weepest thou? Whom seekest thou?"

She thought as she looked through her tears that it must be the man who kept the garden, so she said,

"Sir, if thou have borne Him hence tell me where thou hast laid Him, and I will take Him away."

"Mary!"

It was the voice of Jesus—the same that once said to her, "Thy sins are forgiven," and she spread her arms to clasp His feet, crying.

"*Rabboni!*—my Master!"

"Touch me not," He said, "for I am not yet ascended to my Father:

THE ANGEL OF THE RESURRECTION.

but go to my brethren and say unto them, 'I ascend unto my Father and your Father: and to my God and your God.'"

It was while Mary Magdalene and Mary the mother of James, were still in the garden, perhaps, that Jesus met them and said,

"All hail!" and they fell at His feet and worshipped Him.

"Be not afraid," He said, "go tell my brethren that they go into Galilee and there shall they see me."

When the women told all these things to the apostles who had come together to mourn for their dead Master, they could not believe. But the first Easter had risen upon the world, and though the joy of it filled all heaven, only a few women knew the blessed secret on earth, and were saying over and over, "The Lord is risen! the Lord is risen indeed!"

CHAPTER XLV.

THE EVENING OF EASTER.

It was the afternoon of the same day in which the women had brought such strange stories from the tomb of the buried Christ, that two disciples went out to their home at Emmaus, a village about eight miles from Jerusalem. They had been in the upper room where they often gathered, and had heard the stories of Mary Magdalene, and of Peter and John, and they knew not what to believe.

As Cleopas and his companion (Luke, perhaps) went westward over the hills they talked of all these strange things with bowed heads and sad hearts, for Jesus, the One whom they had trusted was the Redeemer of Israel, was crucified, dead and buried, and as for the words of these women, they seemed like idle tales; but what if they should be true?

Another step seemed to fall beside theirs, and looking up they saw a noble looking young Stranger who was following the same road. He greeted them and said,

"What manner of communications are these that ye have one to another as ye walk, and are sad?"

"Art thou only a stranger in Jerusalem," Cleopas said, "and hast not known the things that are come to pass there in these days?"

"What things?" asked the Stranger, and they said, "Concerning Jesus of Nazareth, which was a prophet mighty in deed and word before God and

THE WALK TO EMMAUS.

all the people, and how the chief priests and our rulers delivered Him to be condemned to death, and have crucified Him. But we trusted that it had been He which should have redeemed Israel : and besides all this to-day is the third day since these things were done."

Cleopas also told the story of the women who had come from the sepulchre that morning talking of a vision of angels, with that of Peter and John, who had gone also, and found it even as the women had said.

Then the Stranger began to speak to them of many things, and in words so full of wisdom and love and faith that their hearts were drawn with Him to believe that Jesus had risen from the dead. He told them that they were very foolish and slow of heart to believe all that the prophets had spoken. "Ought not Christ to have suffered these things," He said, "and to enter into His glory ;" and He explained to them all the Scriptures that foretold the coming, the suffering, and the death of the Messiah, until the two hours' walk seemed as nothing.

As they came to the village where they lived, and the Stranger was passing on, they urged Him to come with them into the low white house near by which was the house of one of them. "Abide with us," they said, "for it is toward evening, and the day is far spent." And He went with them, and sat down with them to their evening meal.

Then another and strange beautiful vision was given at the sunset of the first Easter Day, like that which was given to the women at its dawn. The Stranger took bread and blessed it and broke it, and as He handed it to each disciple their eyes were opened, and they knew Him. It was the Lord! But in a moment He had vanished from their sight, and they could only wonder and believe. They began to recall His words. "Did not our hearts burn within us while He talked with us by the way, and while He opened to us the Scriptures?"

Perhaps they ate the bread that He had broken as they would take the sacrament, and then rose, though the day was fading over the hills of Ephraim and hurried back to Jerusalem to the friend's house where the disciples met. There in the upper room, the doors closed and guarded for fear of the Jews, they told the story of the Stranger to the eager disciples, and found that the Lord had also appeared to Peter.

In the midst of the joy and the wonder there fell a strange hush over the little company, for suddenly the Lord was seen standing in the midst and they heard the greeting so dear and familiar to them all.

" Peace be unto you!" and to them all He spread His hands having the print of the nails in them, and showed them His side that bore the mark of the Roman spear. That they might be still more sure He was the Lord and Master they had loved and followed (for they were afraid), He asked them to touch him; and as they had been at supper together He asked to share their meal, and He ate of the broiled fish and of the honey-comb before them. After this He talked lovingly with them of Himself—of the fulfillment of the prophecies concerning Him and of the work of the kingdom that was before them. Again he blessed them, and breathed on them, saying, "Receive ye the Holy Ghost." And so ended the day of the Lord's resurrection from the dead—the first Easter of the Christian Church.

CHAPTER XLVI.

THE LORD'S LAST DAYS WITH HIS DISCIPLES.

On Easter evening, when the Lord's friends were gathered in the upper room where He appeared to them, one of the eleven was absent. There were others beside the apostles—Cleopas and his companion, and probably the women of Galilee, as well as Mary, and Martha, and Lazarus of Bethany, but Thomas was not there. The others had told him that the Lord had shown Himself to them and had broken bread with them, but he could not believe. He believed, perhaps, in a vision, but not in the return of the crucified Jesus. He declared,

"Except I shall see in His hands the print of the nails, and put my finger into the print of the nails, and thrust my hand into His side, I will not believe."

A week passed, and the disciples were again gathered in the upper room, and Thomas was with them. The doors were shut and guarded as before, but, as before the Lord suddenly stood in the midst, saying,

"Peace be unto you." Then He turned to Thomas with gentle rebuke,

"Reach hither thy finger, and behold my hands; and reach hither thy hand and thrust it into my side, and be not faithless but believing." Thomas did not wait to touch the Lord, but cried,

"My Lord and my God!"

"Thomas," He said, "because thou hast seen me thou hast believed; blessed are they that have not seen and have believed."

Soon after this the apostles went away into Galilee, as the Lord had commanded them to do. There by the Lake where He had called them from their nets to follow Him they waited for Him. Peter, and James, and John were there, with Thomas, and Nathanael, and two others of His disciples. The old love for the Lake came back to Peter, and he said,

"I go a fishing," and the others said,

"We also go with thee," and they went out for a night with the nets on the Lake, but they caught nothing. In the morning as they drew a little nearer land they saw a dim figure on the shore and heard a voice saying to them,

"Children, have ye any meat?" They answered "No," and then the clear voice came across the water saying,

"Cast the net on the right side of the ship, and ye shall find." This they did, and so heavy did the net become with fishes that they were not able to draw it. Perhaps John remembered another day on the Lake when the nets broke with the weight of the fishes, and looking at the figure standing on the shore in the sunrise, he said to Peter,

"It is the Lord!"

Peter did not wait to reply, but tying his fisher's coat around him he threw himself into the Lake to swim towards His Master on the shore. The others followed in the ship dragging the net with them, and when they had landed they found a fire of coals there, with fish laid upon it and bread, and the Lord Himself standing there as one who served.

"Bring of the fish ye have now caught," He said. And Peter, first to obey, drew the net to land full of great fishes—one hundred and fifty-three—and the net was not broken. While they were silent for joy and wonder, knowing that it was the Lord, and yet not daring to question Him, He said, "Come and dine." And there upon the sands the Lord for the third time since He rose from the dead, broke bread with his disciples. John, the beloved disciple was there, but it is not recorded that Jesus spoke to him personally. His heart was wholly with his Lord, and he did not need the loving help that was given to doubting Thomas, and self-confident, wavering Peter. To Simon Peter He said after they had finished their simple meal,

"Simon, son of Jonas, lovest thou me more than these?"

Peter must have remembered that he had vehemently declared, "Although *all* shall be offended, yet will not I. If I should die with Thee yet I will not deny Thee in any wise," and had straightway forsaken and denied Him. Now he said simply and humbly,

"Yea, Lord: Thou knowest that I love Thee." And the Lord answered, "Feed my lambs."

THE ASCENSION.

Again the Lord asked him the same question, and Peter gave the same reply. And the Lord said, "Feed my sheep."

When the Lord had asked this question the third time, Peter, full of love and grief cried,

"Lord, Thou knowest all things: Thou knowest that I love thee." And the Lord answered again, "Feed my sheep."

By this Peter knew that the Lord trusted him to be an apostle, and teach the gospel of the kingdom to all men, but that he must have a steadfast love and faith. The Lord also said, "When thou wast young thou guidedst thyself, and walkest whither thou wouldest; but when thou shalt be old thou shalt stretch forth thy hands and another shall guide thee, and carry thee whither thou wouldest not." Afterward Peter was crucified as his Lord had been, and then John remembered these words of the Lord about him. As the Lord said to Peter, "Follow me," Peter saw John following also, and he said, wondering, perhaps, why the Lord had no word of counsel, of rebuke, or of prophecy for John,

"Lord, and what shall this man do?" And Jesus replied, "If I will that he tarry till I come, what is that to thee? Follow thou me." And they went away from the Lake, following the Lord, as they had done three years before when He called them to be "fishers of men."

CHAPTER XLVII.

"HE ASCENDED INTO HEAVEN."

Once more the Lord met His little company of followers and gave the apostles authority to found the Kingdom of God among men. "All power has been given to me," He said, "in heaven and on earth."

And this was the work that He gave them to do: "Go ye therefore and teach all nations, baptizing them in the name of the Father, and of the Son, and of the Holy Ghost: teaching them to observe all things whatsoever I have commanded you."

And this was His true word of promise to them: "Lo I am with you always, even unto the end of the world. And, behold, I send the promise of my Father upon you: but tarry ye in the city of Jerusalem until ye be endued with power from on high."

It was about six weeks after His death that the disciples were again in

Jerusalem where the Lord had told them to go and wait for the coming of His Spirit. He led them out over the Mount of Olives as far as Bethany, where the house of Martha had been a place of rest and refreshment for the homeless Man of Sorrows while He was founding His Kingdom of Heaven on the earth.

As they ascended a hill just above Bethany, the Lord could see spread out before Him the Hebron hills toward Bethlehem where He was born: the great city with its golden Temple where He had taught and had been rejected; Gethsemane, where He had suffered, and had been betrayed; and beyond the western walls the place where He had been crucified. Not far from Golgotha was the garden and the tomb in which He had been buried, and from which He had risen.

He was about to leave the little group that He had made the founders of His Kingdom, and one of them ventured a question,

"Lord, wilt thou at this time restore again the Kingdom to Israel?" And the Lord replied,

"It is not for you to know the time and the seasons, which the Father hath put in His own power. But ye shall be witnesses unto me both in Jerusalem, and in all Judea, and in Samaria, and unto the uttermost parts of the earth."

Then He blessed them, and while they were looking at Him He was lifted above them, and a cloud seemed to come between them and their Divine Master.

While they still gazed toward heaven hoping perhaps to see Him again, two men in white garments stood by them and said,

"Ye men of Galilee, why stand ye gazing up into heaven? This same Jesus, which is taken up from you into heaven, shall so come in like manner as ye have seen Him go into heaven."

Then they worshipped their ascended Lord, and returned to Jerusalem full of joy and praise, to meet the other disciples in the upper room, to tell them of what they had seen, and to wait for the Promise of the Father.

CHAPTER XLVIII.

THE PROMISE OF THE FATHER.

While the disciples of Jesus waited in Jerusalem for the gift of the Holy Spirit—the Comforter—who was to come and teach them all things, and bring all the Lord's words to their remembrance, they were much in prayer, and looked to the Lord for direction about the things of the Kingdom.

Peter did much to help the others, for his faith had grown stronger, and he was no longer afraid. Many who had partly believed in Jesus before His crucifixion, and who had come to believe in the risen Lord, joined the little band, until they numbered one hundred and twenty at one of their meetings, and the mother of Jesus was among them. At this meeting Peter proposed that some disciple who could be a witness with them to the Lord's resurrection should be appointed to the place that Judas once held in the circle of the twelve. The ten disciples agreed with Peter, and two were chosen—Joseph and Matthias. Then they prayed that the Lord Himself would show them which of these two He wished to be an Apostle, and when they cast lots the lot fell upon Matthias.

When the upper room became too small they went to a larger one that was more public, and did not try to guard their doors, for the priests had become afraid of the people as well as of the signs at the time of the Lord's death, when the sky was darkened, the rocks rent by an earthquake, and the Temple veil by an unseen Hand.

The Feast of the Weeks came on, and at the end of May—the day of Pentecost (the fiftieth after the second day of the Passover), the Lord's little church had gathered in their large public room to pray and wait for the Promise. Suddenly there came a sound from the heavens like the rushing of a mighty wind, and with it came a flash of fire which was not lightning, but which divided into many, and sat above the brow of each like a soft, bright tongue of flame.

Then the silence was broken, and they all began to praise God in other languages, as the Spirit gave them utterance, for the Promise of the Father had been given, and the Lord Himself had come to dwell in His people—not only in these, but in all who should believe on Him through their word.

There were some good Jews present who had come from foreign countries to the Feast, and spoke other languages, and when each heard his own language spoken by these unlearned men they were astonished. The news spread and many came to hear. "Are not all these which speak Galileans?" they asked, "and how hear we every man in our own tongue wherein we were born? What meaneth this?" Others made light of it all, and said that they were full of new wine.

Then Peter, strong in the power of the Holy Spirit, stood up and spoke to the people. You will find Peter's sermon in the second chapter of Acts, and his text was a wonderful saying of the prophet Joel, beginning, as Peter gave it,—

"And it shall come to pass in the last days I will pour out of my Spirit upon all flesh: and your sons and your daughters shall prophesy, and your young men shall dream dreams; and on my servants, and on my handmaidens I will pour out in those days of my Spirit; and they shall prophesy. And it shall come to pass that whosoever shall call on the name of the Lord shall be saved."

Peter did not spare the enemies of our Lord in his sermon, nor did he fear them. He preached to them of Jesus of Nazareth, and whom they had taken and by wicked hands had crucified and slain; and whom God had raised up, having loosed the pains of death, because it was not possible that He should be holden of it. He closed by telling them that God had made that same Jesus whom they had crucified both Lord and Christ.

There were many among the people gathered there who were pricked in their hearts because of Peter's words, which had the power of the Holy Spirit in them. They looked at each other and said,

"Men and brethren, what shall we do?"

Peter encouraged them to repentance and baptism in the name of Jesus Christ, telling them that the promise was to them and to their children, and to all that were afar off.

It was a wonderful day for the Church of Jesus Christ, and for His Kingdom on the earth, for there were about three thousand who that day received baptism, and joined the little despised company of the followers of Jesus of Nazareth. And all that believed were drawn together by the love of the Lord Jesus, and no longer lived for themselves, but for each other. That there might be no rich and no poor among them, they sold their possessions and parted them to all, as every one had need. In the Temple, in each other's houses breaking bread together, wherever they were they were happy and strong in their new faith and in favor with all the people. Though great trials and persecutions came after awhile, they bore them as seeing their invisible Lord, and they joyfully met the loss of all things—even that of life itself with a smile, remembering the Father's House with its many mansions, and their spiritual Elder Brother who had gone to prepare a place for them.

AN AFTERWORD.

Dear Child:—God's Book is a Book of Ages, a Book of Races, and a Book of Nations; but it is far more, it is a Book through which God Himself speaks to the soul of man. We begin to read it thinking that He is speaking to the mind; afterward, when our conscience wakes, we believe He speaks to the heart, but at last we find that He speaks to the inmost spirit—the immortal soul. Then all that had seemed to be history, poetry, biography, philosophy, begins to be to us the voice of God in the inmost of the soul, speaking of the life of the spirit.

We find at last, too, that One has walked beside us all the way, teaching us by His Spirit as He taught the people on the hill-side, or by the lake-side in Galilee: the One who said, "Before Abraham was, I am"—the Child of Bethlehem, whose name was called "Wonderful, Counsellor, The Mighty God, the Everlasting Father, The Prince of Peace." That you, dear child, may find Him walking close beside your way, be in the habit of walking daily with Him in the paths of His Word, and He will reveal Himself to you there.

www.ingramcontent.com/pod-product-compliance
Lightning Source LLC
Chambersburg PA
CBHW030352170426
43202CB00010B/1350